UNDERSTANDING CONNECTIVITY

IN

NIKON Z9

MIRRORLESS CAMERA

Joe Smith

Copyright 2022 © Joe Smith

All rights reserved. This book is copyright and no part of it may be reproduced, stored or transmitted, in any form or means, without the prior written permission of the copyright owner.

Printed in the United States of America

Copyright 2022 © Joe Smith.

Contents

Introduction 1

Connecting your camera to HDMI devices 2

    TVs 3

    Recorder 3

    Modifying the Settings 4

    Output Resolution 6

    External Recording Control 9

    Connect to your smart devices 10

    The SnapBridge Application 10

    Features and Benefits of SnapBridge 11

    Importing Photographs from a Camera 11

    Remote photography 12

    Wireless Connections 12

    Pairing-connect with Bluetooth 12

    Pairing 12

    Connect to Smart Device Previously-Paired 16

    Employing a wireless network connection (Wi-Fi Mode) 16

    Connecting 16

    Make the Connection 20

    Computers: Connect with USB cable 21

    Computers: Connect with Ethernet or with Wireless LAN 22

    FTP Servers: Connecting with Ethernet or with Wireless LAN 23

    Computers: Connecting with USB cable 23

    Install NX Studio 24

Transferring Photographs Using NX Studio 25

Connect your camera to a laptop or desktop. 25

Using a Card Reader 26

Turn on your camera 26

Computers: Connect with Ethernet or with Wireless LAN 28

The Benefits of Wired and Wireless Local Area Networking 28

Uploading Pictures 28

Remotely Control your Camera 29

Wireless Transmitting Utility 30

Wireless LAN 31

Direct Wireless Connectivity (Mode-Access-Point) 31

Infrastructure-mode connectivity 43

Infrastructure mode 44

Easy Connect 46

Ethernet Connection 57

Connect Ethernet Cable 57

Profiles in Ethernet Network 58

Uploading Pictures 69

Real-time image uploading 72

Upload Icon 73

Camera Control 76

End your Camera and computer Connection 80

FTP Servers: Connecting through Ethernet or through Wireless LAN 80

Wireless LAN 81

Direct Wireless Connect (Access-Point) 81

Create host profile with cam-connection wizard 82

Manual Configuration 84

Firewall Settings 90

Connect in Infrastructure Mode 92

Infrastructure mode 92

Easy Connect 96

Firewall Settings 103

Ethernet 105

Connect an Ethernet Plug In 105

Manual Configuration 107

Firewall Settings 114

Uploading Pictures 115

Troubleshoot Ethernet and Wireless LAN Connections 117

   Problems and Solution 117

Error Codes 118

Wireless Error 119

[TCP/IP Error.] 120

[PTP/IP Error.] 121

[FTP Error.] 121

Camera to camera connection 122

Camera Remote Photography (Sync Release) 122

Clock Sync (Date & Time) 123

Configure and use Sync Release 124

Wireless LAN 124

Easy Connect 127

Add the other remote camera 136

Take pictures. 137

Ethernet 137

Flash Photography 145

   "On-Camera" Vs "Remote" 145

Mounted Camera Flash Units 145

Remote Flash Photography 146

Use On-Camera Flash 147

Flash Control Mode 148

Flash Modes 151

FV Lock 153

Focus 154

Lock flash level. 155

Remove the FV Lock 156

Introduction

Welcome to Nikon Z9 simplified user guide. This user guide is centred on the Nikon Z9 connectivity. How to connect other HTML smart devices to the camera, connect camera to camera and other connections.

Many people are talking about the Nikon Z9 right now. We talk about the Z9, which is one of the most interesting camera we've seen in a long time.

As you might expect, the quality of the build is great. It's easy to hold because the grips give your fingers a lot of room in both directions and the buttons are very close to your hand.

The LCD screen on the back doesn't move all the way around just similar to other cameras. In fact, it's a lot like the S1 in tilting it up, down, and towards your right, but you can't put it in a selfie position. You might wonder its importance on a professional camera, but if you wish to shoot your own videos from the tripod, then it can be of great help to have.

Connecting your camera to HDMI devices

The camera may be connected to HDMI-enabled televisions, recorders, and other HDMI-enabled devices. Use an HDMI cable from a third-party manufacturer. The cable is not included in the package. Before adding or removing a cable, make sure the camera is turned off.

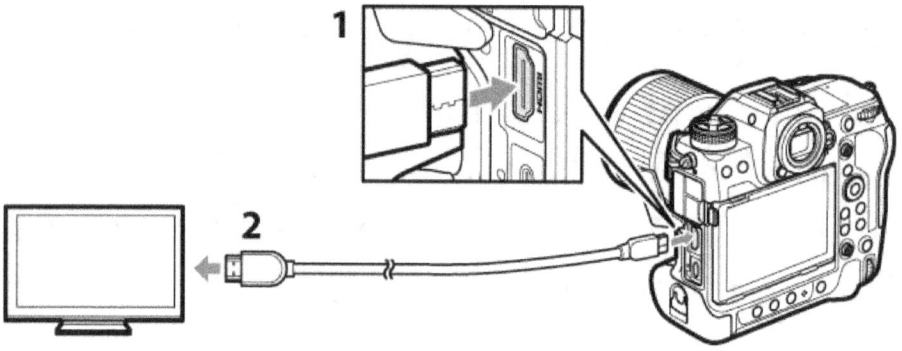

1. HDMI connector used for connecting to your camera device

2. HDMI connector used for connecting to external devices.

Select an HDMI cable that has a connection that is compatible with the HDMI device.

TVs

To see images on the television, switch on the camera and click the K button once the TV has been set to HDMI input channel.

The level of the audio being played back may be altered by using the TV's controls. Using the camera controls will not work.

When the camera is connected to a TV through HDMI, the SnapBridge software on a smartphone or tablet may be used in controlling playback from a distance. Visit SnapBridge's support site for further information.

Connect 8K-capable TVs with an HDMI input connection that complies with HDMI 2.1.

Recorder

When in the video mode, your camera may record straight to HDMI recorders connected to the camera.

If you insert a memory card into the camera while it is connected to the recorder, video would be recorded to both the memory card and recorder. If you didn't insert any memory card, the video will only be saved on the external device.

Modifying the Settings

Adjusting the parameters for HDMI output may be done using the [HDMI] item in setup menu.

Option	Description
[Output resolution]	The format for output to HDMI devices can be selected from [Auto], [4320p (progressive)], [2160p (progressive)], [1080p (progressive)], and [720p (progressive)].
[Output range]	The RGB video signal input range varies with the HDMI device. [Auto], which matches the output range to the HDMI device, is recommended in most situations. If the camera is unable to determine the correct RGB video signal output range for the HDMI device, you can choose from the following options:

Option	Description
	- [Limited range]: For devices with an RGB video signal input range of 16 to 235. Choose this option if you notice a loss of detail in shadows. - [Full range]: For devices with an RGB video signal input range of 0 to 255. Choose this option if you notice that shadows are "washed out" or too bright.
[Output shooting info]	Choose whether shooting information is displayed on the HDMI device. If [ON] is selected, icons and other information in the shooting display will be recorded with the footage saved to external recorders.

Option	Description
[Mirror camera info display]	Choose whether the display in the camera monitor remains on while an HDMI device is connected. • If [OFF] is selected, the display will remain off, reducing the drain on the camera battery. • [Mirror camera info display] will be fixed at [ON] while [OFF] is selected for [Output shooting info].

Output Resolution

In the setup menu, selecting [Auto] for the [HDMI] > [Output resolution] option allows the camera to automatically determine whether or not external recorder allows the rate and frame size that has been specified on the camera. In the event that it does not, the camera will perform the searches for a compatible resolution as well as frame rate in the sequence shown below. If it is determined that the requested resolution or frame rate are not supported, the output will be stopped.

- If no card was inserted into the camera:

Frame size/frame rate	Output resolution/frame rate search order
[7680×4320; 30p]	4320/30p V 2160/30p V 1080/30p
[7680×4320; 25p]	4320/25p V 2160/25p V 1080/25p
[7680×4320; 24p]	4320/24p V 2160/24p V 1080/24p
[3840×2160; 120p]	2160/120p V 1080/120p V 2160/60p V 1080/60p V 2160/30p V 1080/30p
[3840×2160; 100p]	2160/100p V 1080/100p V 2160/50p V 1080/50p V 2160/25p V 1080/25p
[3840×2160; 60p]	2160/60p V 1080/60p V 2160/30p V 1080/30p
[3840×2160; 50p]	2160/50p V 1080/50p V 2160/25p V 1080/25p
[3840×2160; 30p]	2160/30p V 1080/30p
[3840×2160; 25p]	2160/25p V 1080/25p
[3840×2160; 24p]	2160/24p V 1080/24p
[1920×1080; 120p]	1080/120p V 1080/60p V 1080/30p

[1920×1080; 100p]	1080/100p V 1080/50p V 1080/25p
[1920×1080; 60p]	1080/60p V 1080/30p
[1920×1080; 50p]	1080/50p V 1080/25p
[1920×1080; 30p]	1080/30p
[1920×1080; 25p]	1080/25p
[1920×1080; 24p]	1080/24p

- Memory card is inserted into the camera:

Frame size/frame rate	Output resolution/frame rate search order
[7680×4320; 30p]	1080/30p
[7680×4320; 25p]	1080/25p
[7680×4320; 24p]	1080/24p
[3840×2160; 120p]	1080/60p V 1080/30p
[3840×2160; 100p]	1080/50p V 1080/25p
[3840×2160; 60p]–[1920×1080; 24p]	Same as when no memory card is inserted in the camera.

When a resolution besides [Auto] is chosen for [Output res.], the signal is output at that resolution. If one of the following conditions are met, HDMI output will be halted:

- The output resolution must be larger than the currently used frame size.
- The recorder is not compatible with the chosen output resolution

External Recording Control

By switching [External rec. ctrl (HDMI)] to [ON] in the video recording menu, users may utilize the camera's controls to initiate and stop recording on an external recorder.

Whether you want to know if your recorder can be controlled from a distance, it's best to ask the people who made it.

When the time in Custom Settings c3 [Power off delay] > [Standby timer] elapses, HDMI output from the camera will be cut off automatically. Select [Standby timer] then set it to [No limit] or a duration greater than the expected recording time when saving films to an external device.

When [ON] is activated, the following symbol will appear on the camera monitor: If no video is being captured at the time, option A will be shown, but option B will be active. If you want to be sure your recording is really getting stored to the device, check recorder and the recorder's display as you go.

Choosing [ON] may cause the device's video output to become garbled, so be careful.

Connect to your smart devices

The SnapBridge Application

Connect your camera to your mobile device ("smart device") wirelessly with the help of the SnapBridge software.

The SnapBridge app is available for free on both the iTunes App Store and the Google Play Store.

If you want to know what's happening with SnapBridge, go over to Nikon's website.

SnapBridge may provide you with a licensing agreement or similar screen upon startup; please read it carefully and continue only if you agree to its terms.

Features and Benefits of SnapBridge

Below, we've detailed the many functions that may be achieved with the help of the SnapBridge app. See the SnapBridge app's online documentation for further information:

https://nikonimglib.com/snbr/onlinehelp/en/index.html

Importing Photographs from a Camera

Get some photographs off the internet and onto your mobile device. As they are being taken, they may be instantly downloaded.

Remote photography

Use the smart smartphone as a remote control for the camera and to snap images.

Wireless Connections

Connect the camera to your smartphone wirelessly with the help of the SnapBridge app. Both Bluetooth and Wi-Fi may be used to establish a connection; see "Connecting through Bluetooth (Pairing)" and "Connecting via Wi-Fi (Wi-Fi Mode)," respectively. Using Bluetooth to link devices enables instantaneous photo uploads straight from the camera.

Pairing-connect with Bluetooth

The camera & smart device must be paired before the first Bluetooth connection can be made.

Pairing

Follow these steps to link your camera to your mobile device.

The camera is used for certain tasks, while the smart device is used for others.

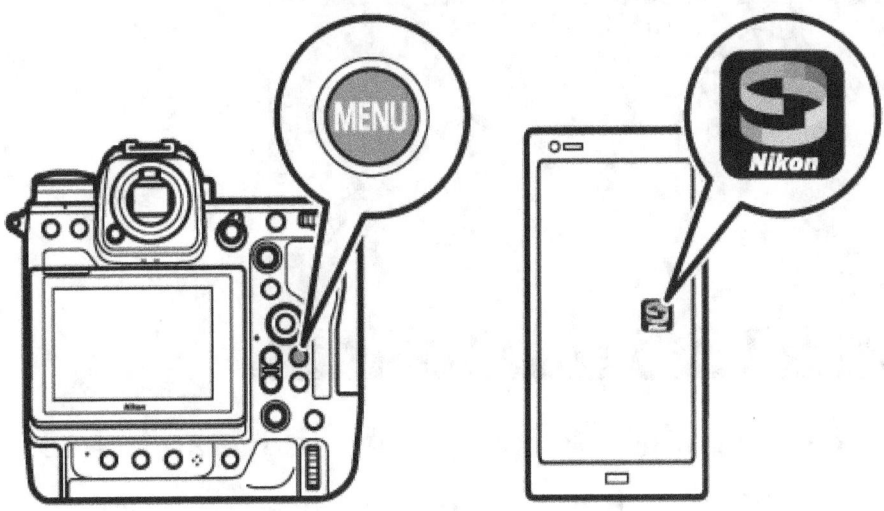

SnapBridge's online documentation provides more guidance.

Camera: In the network menu, go to [Connect to your smart device] > [Pairing (Bluetooth)], tap [Start pairing], and then click J.

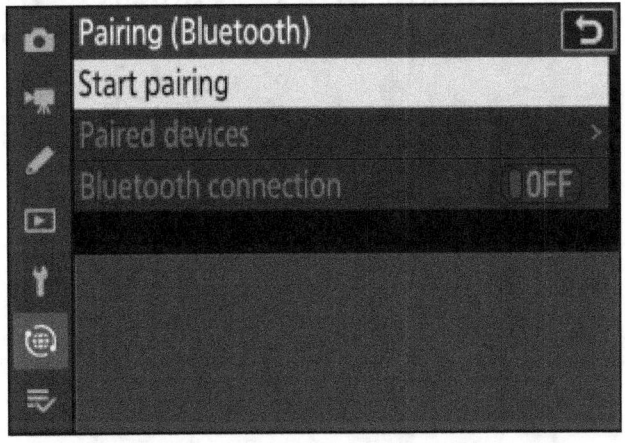

The monitor will show the camera's name.

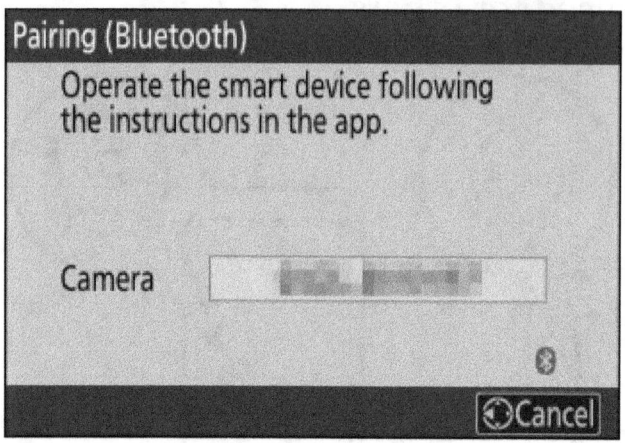

A clever gadget: Start up SnapBridge and choose [Connect to camera] from the menu.

When starting the app for the first time, choose [Connect to camera] from the first screen.

Follow the on-screen prompts to use your smart device.

Select the "pairing" option when requested to select the kind of connection, then hit the "category" button for your camera.

When asked, choose the camera by tapping its name.

Follow the on-screen prompts on both the camera and the smart device to finish pairing after you've verified that they're showing the same authentication code.

To start the connection between your smart device and camera, click the J button on camera and then tap the pairing button on your smart device.

As soon as the camera & smart device are paired, a confirmation message will appear on both. After that, the camera will go straight to its menus without your intervention.

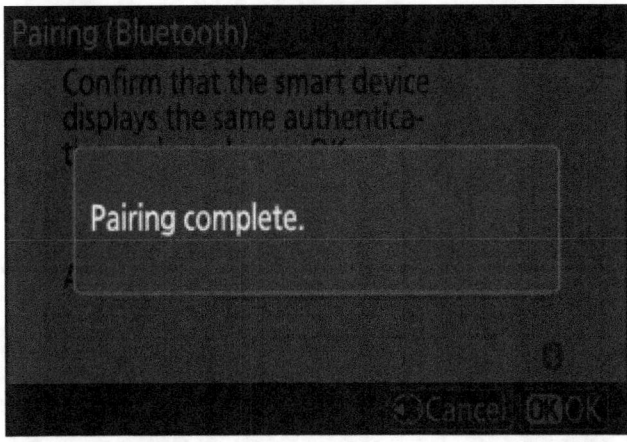

The camera and smart device are now paired.

For information on using the SnapBridge app, see online help.

Connect to Smart Device Previously-Paired

Simply turning on Bluetooth on smart device & camera and opening the SnapBridge app will allow you to connect after they have been matched.

Employing a wireless network connection (Wi-Fi Mode)

When set to Wi-Fi mode, camera establishes an instantaneous wireless connection with the smart device without the need to first pair the devices through Bluetooth.

Connecting

In order to set up a wireless connection between your camera and smart device, please refer to the instructions below.

The camera is used for certain tasks, while the smart device is used for others.

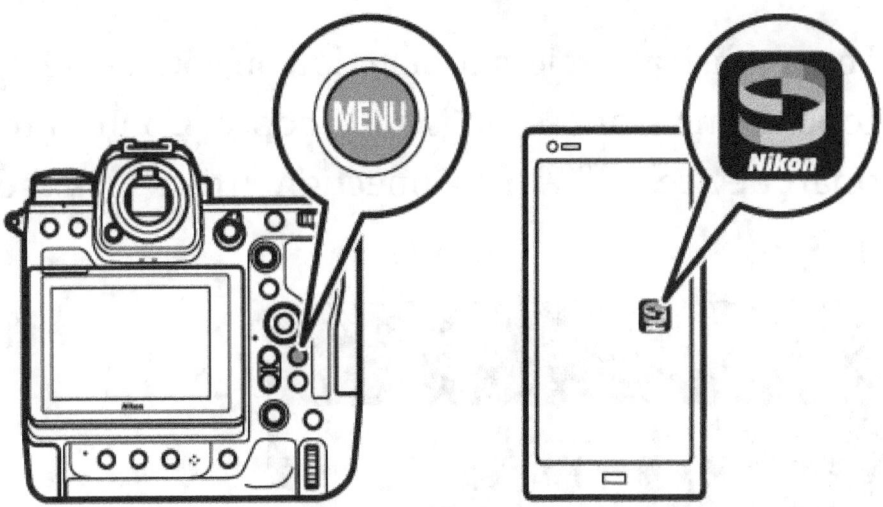

SnapBridge's online documentation provides more guidance.

Smart device: Get the SnapBridge application going by opening the ◉ tab, tapping ✱, and choosing [Wi-Fi mode].

If this is your first time using the application, you should choose [Connect to camera] from the welcome screen. Choose the "Wi Fi" option when requested, then press the category for the camera.

If you are using a camera or smart device, activate the camera when requested to do so.

Please refrain from interacting with the app in any way.

To establish a wireless connection on your camera, go to the network settings and choose "Connect to smart device" > "Wi-Fi connection," then click the "J" key.

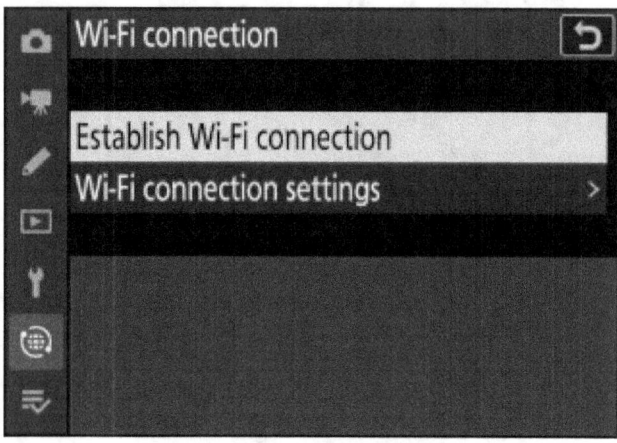

Displayed are the camera's SSID and password.

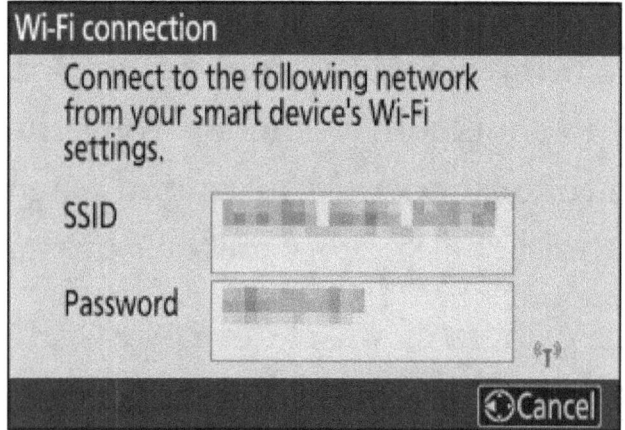

Follow your smart device's on-screen prompts to set up a wireless network connection.

The "Settings" app will open on iOS devices. If you want to change your Wi-Fi settings, you'll need to enter [Settings] by tapping [Settings], then hit [Wi Fi] (which should be at the top of the list)..

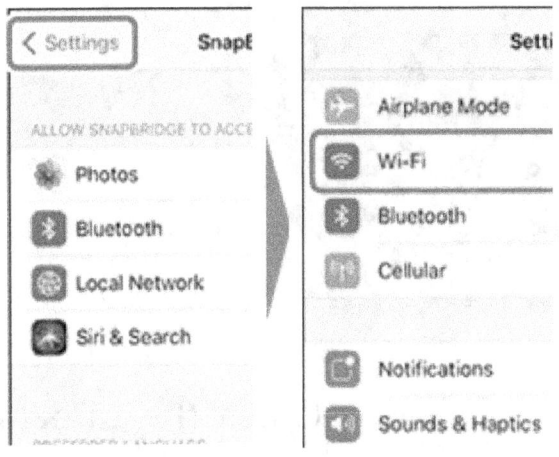

Select the camera's SSID in the Wi-Fi settings menu and input the password shown on the camera's screen at Step 3.

Smart device: Return to SnapBridge application on your smart device after modifying the settings as detailed in Step 4.

Once a wireless connection has been established between the smart device and the camera, a menu of available Wi-Fi settings will appear on the smart device's screen.

After the camera and device are successfully connected, a confirmation message will be shown.

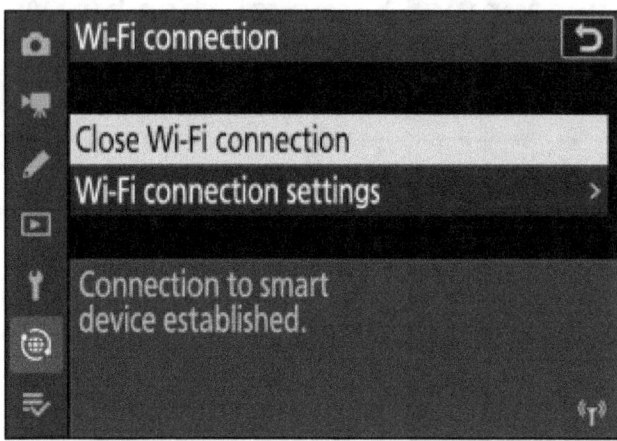

Wi-Fi has been established between the camera and the smart device.

Make the Connection

Any of the following ways may be used to connect the camera to a personal computer or FTP server.

- Computers: Use USB to Connect
- Computers: Connect with Ethernet or with Wireless LAN

- FTP Servers: Connect with Ethernet or with Wireless LAN

Computers: Connect with USB cable

To transfer images from camera to PC, just utilize the USB cable and NX Studio.

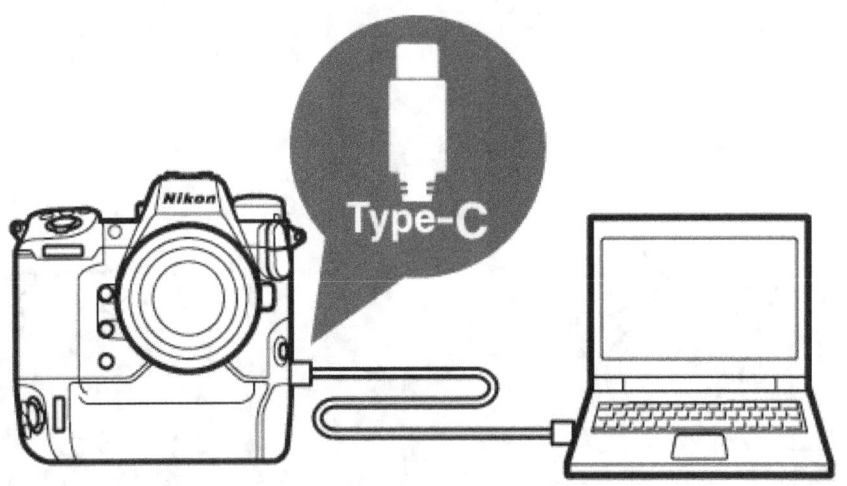

Using the computer and the supplementary program Camera Control Pro 2, you may operate the camera from a distance.

Computers: Connect with Ethernet or with Wireless LAN

Use either the camera's Ethernet port or the wireless LAN functionality to link it to your computer. Using the camera's extra software, Camera Control Pro 2, you may transfer images to your computer or operate the camera via a network.

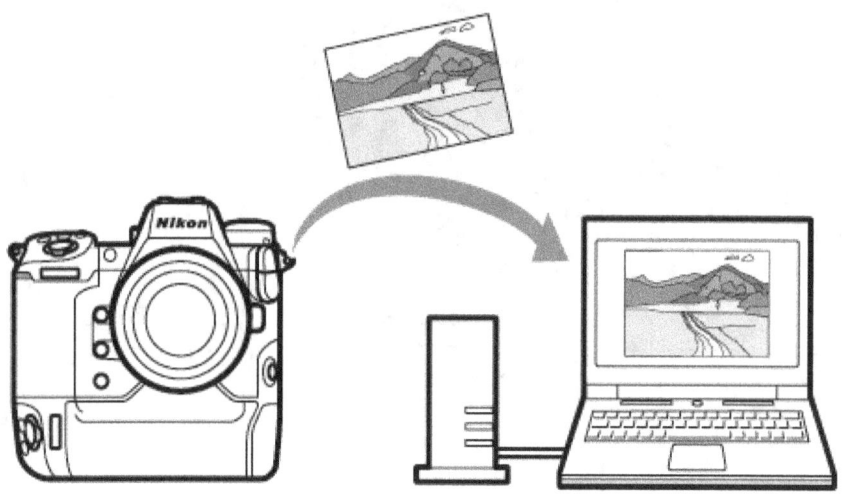

FTP Servers: Connecting with Ethernet or with Wireless LAN

The camera's built-in Ethernet or wireless LAN may be used to transfer images to an FTP server.

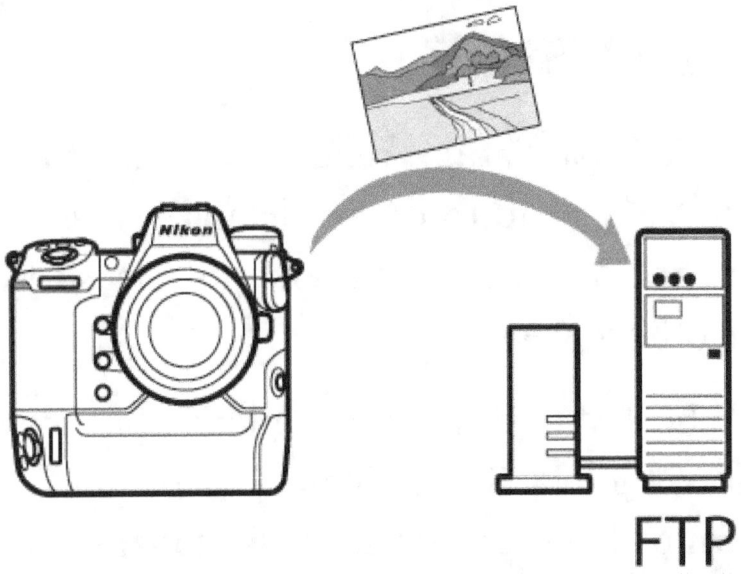

Computers: Connecting with USB cable

Use the USB cord that comes with the camera to link it to your computer. To view and edit your photos later, transfer them to your computer and utilize the NX Studio program.

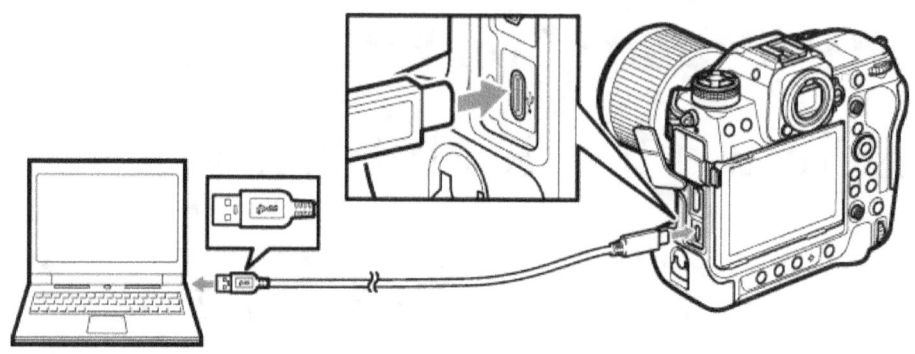

Install NX Studio

NX Studio installation requires access to the Internet. For up-to-date details, including software and hardware requirements, please go to Nikon's official website.

Follow the link below to download the newest version of the NX Studio installer, and then run the downloaded file to finish the installation.

https://downloadcenter.nikonimglib.com/

Keep in mind that older models of NX Studio may be incompatible with the camera's download feature.

Transferring Photographs Using NX Studio

For more clarification, please see the online documentation.

Connect your camera to a laptop or desktop.

After powering off the camera and checking if memory card is installed, attach the wire as indicated.

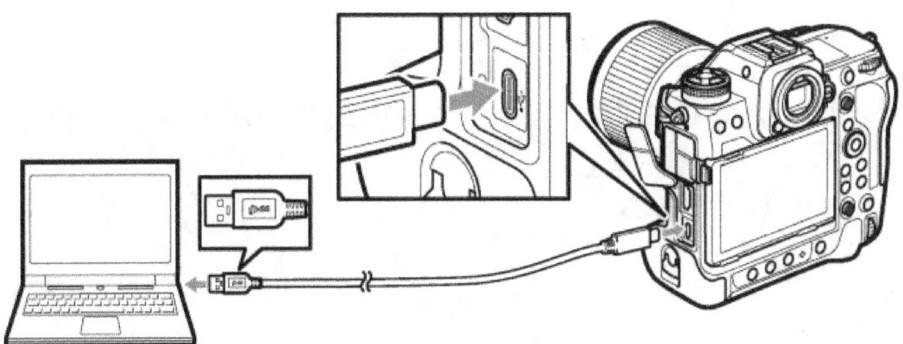

Using a Card Reader

Turn on your camera

Soon, NX Studio's Nikon Transfer 2 feature will begin.

NX Studio includes the Nikon Transfer 2 image-sharing program.

Nikon Transfer 2 should be the app of choice if prompted.

Nikon Transfer 2 should begin loading automatically, but if it doesn't, open NX Studio and choose the "Import" button.

To initiate the transfer, choose [Begin Transfer].

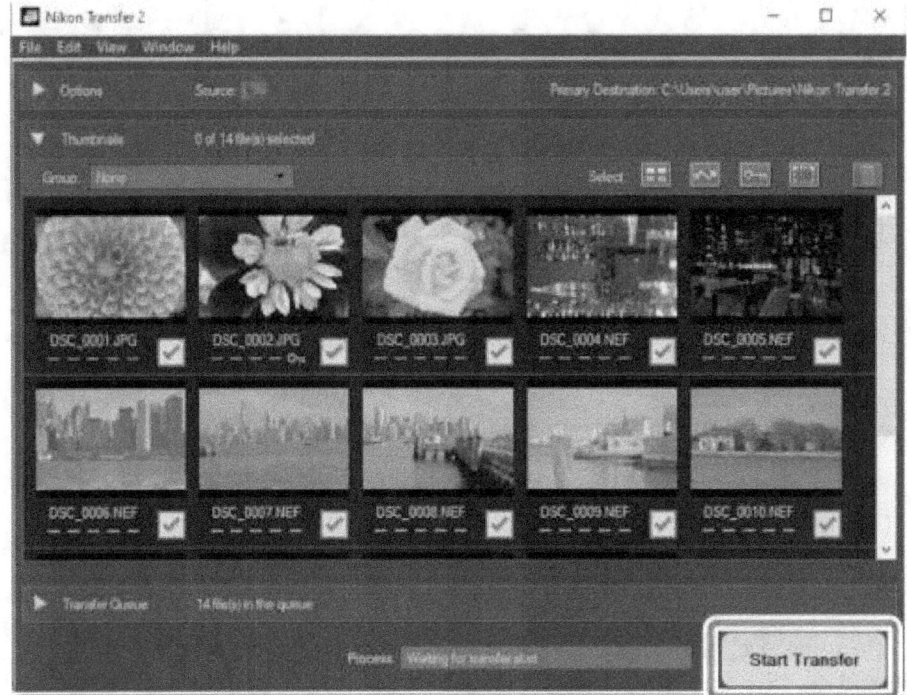

The camera's memory card will have its contents imported into the PC.

Shut off the camera immediately.

When the transfer is finished, remove the USB cord.

Computers: Connect with Ethernet or with Wireless LAN

The camera has an Ethernet port that allows for direct connection to computers or integration into preexisting networks through Wi-Fi (integrated wireless LAN) or an external Ethernet cable.

The Benefits of Wired and Wireless Local Area Networking

A few examples of applications for wireless and wired LAN connections are as follows:

Uploading Pictures

Images already in existence may be transferred digitally. As they are being taken, they may be immediately posted.

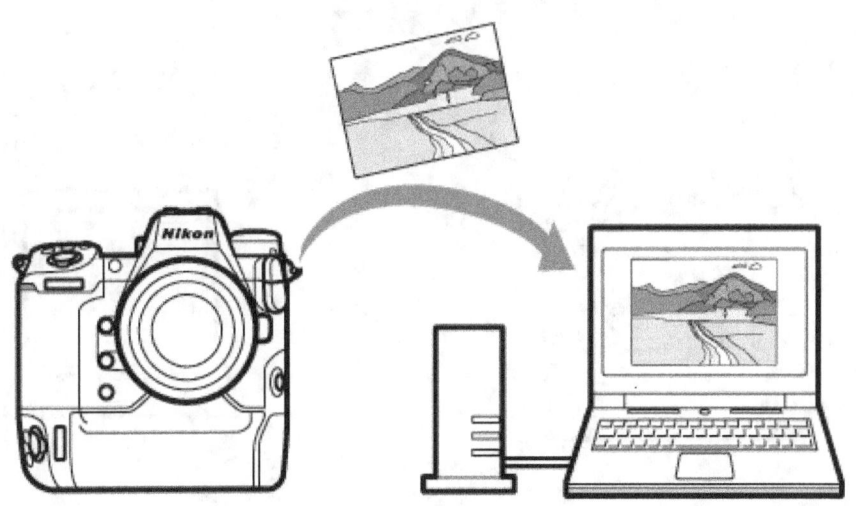

Remotely Control your Camera

Control the exposure and other camera settings remotely by installing Camera Control Pro 2 (purchased individually) on networked computer (Camera Control).

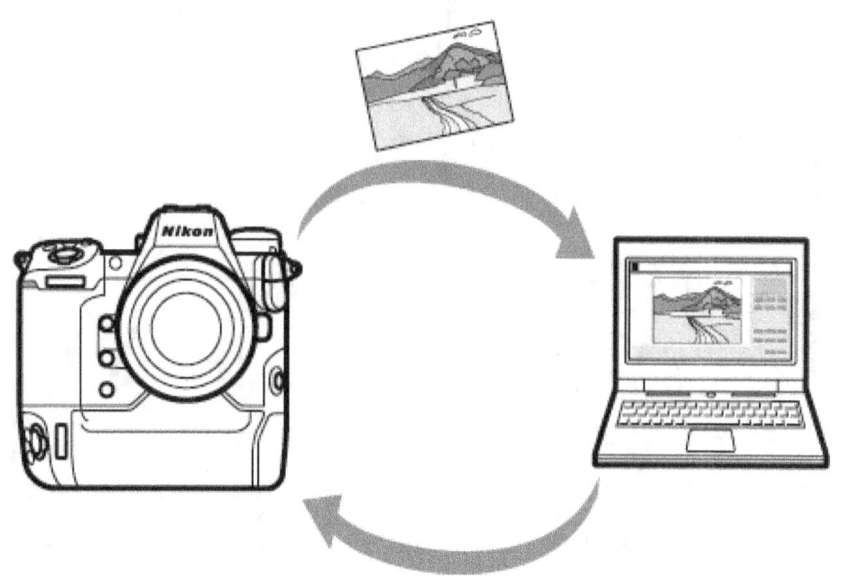

Wireless Transmitting Utility

Nikon's Wireless Transmitter Utility program must be used to link the camera and computer before they may communicate via a wireless or Ethernet LAN.

Camera-to-computer connections are possible after first pairing.

To get the Wireless Transmitter Utility, go on over to the Nikon Download Center. Be sure to get the most recent version by checking the system requirements and version.

https://downloadcenter.nikonimglib.com/

Wireless LAN

The camera is compatible with both direct wireless connection (access-point mode) and indirect wireless connection (through wireless router on existing network, such as home networks) to personal computers (infrastructure mode).

Direct Wireless Connectivity (Mode-Access-Point)

A wireless connection is used to link the camera to the PC. Because of the camera's ability to function as wireless LAN entry point, it may be used to establish a connection even when the pc is not in range of a wireless network. While the camera is linked to the PC, Internet access is unavailable.

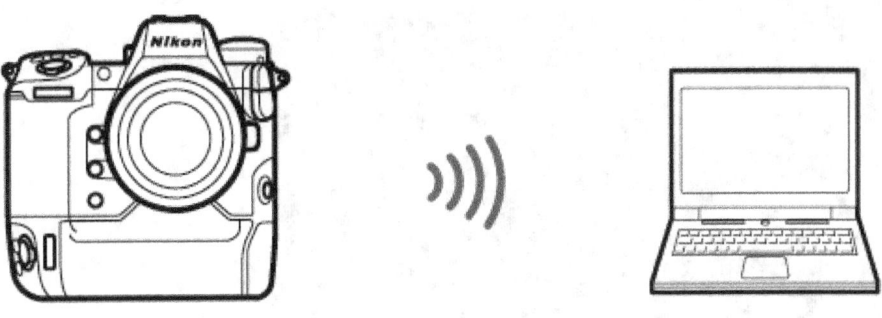

Make sure Wireless Transmitter Utility is present on the PC before continuing.

Make sure the [Wired LAN] option is turned off in the network settings.

In network menu, click "Connect to computer," then "Network settings," and finally "2."

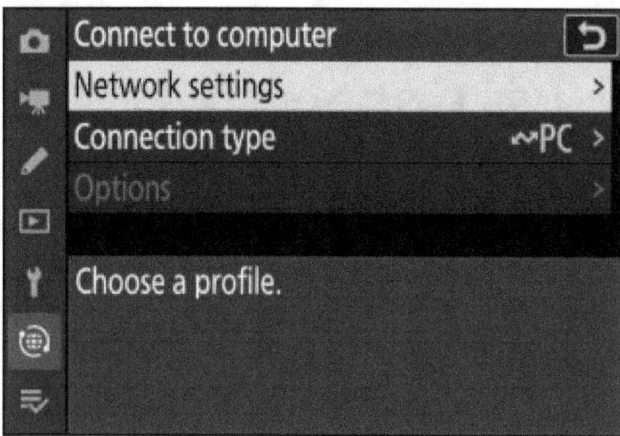

1. Highlight the [Create profile] then tap J.

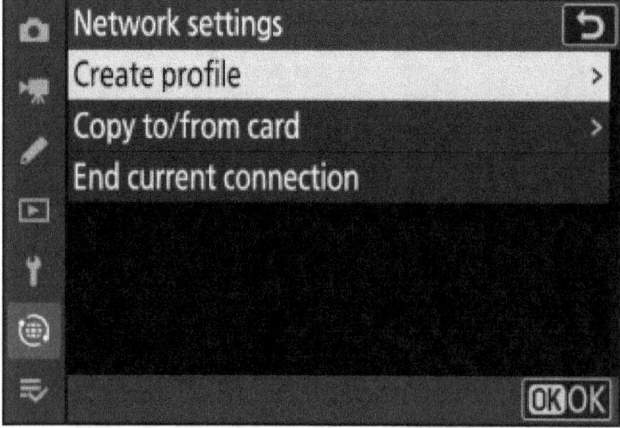

Title the new profile.

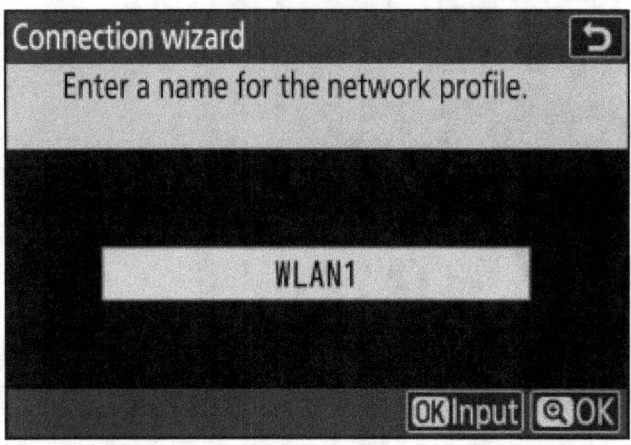

If you're OK with the default name and want to skip this stage, just hit the X.

Whatever you give your network connection will show up under [Connect to the computer] > then [Network settings] in the network menu.

Press J to rename the profile. Please refer to "Text Entry" for details on how to enter text (Text Entry). After a name is entered, press X to continue.

Select "Direct connection to computer" and hit the "J" key to continue.

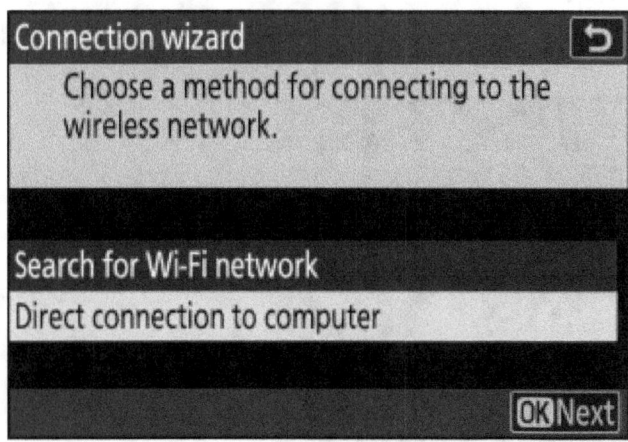

You will then see the device SSID as well as its encryption key.

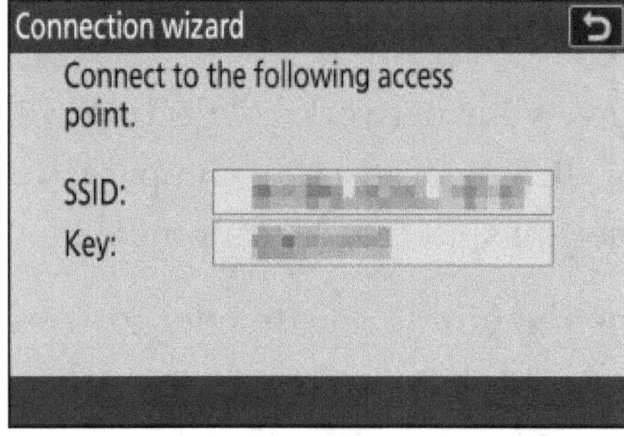

Create a connection with your camera.

On Windows:

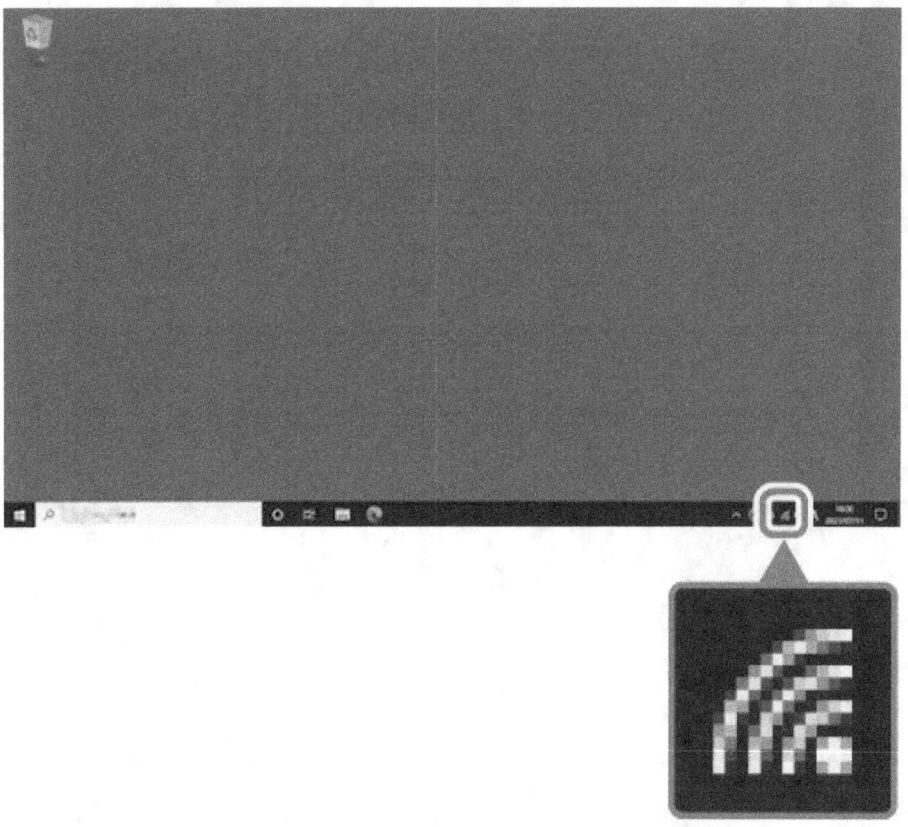

To access a wireless LAN, tap the corresponding icon in the system tray.

In Step 4, choose the SSID that the camera shows.

Input the encryption key shown by the camera in Step 4 when requested to type in network security key. The computer will reach out to the camera and establish contact.

For macOS:

To activate wireless LAN, choose the corresponding menu item.

In Step 4, choose the SSID that the camera shows.

Input the encryption key shown by the camera in Step 4 when requested to input the network security key. The computer will reach out to the camera and establish contact.

Start pairing.

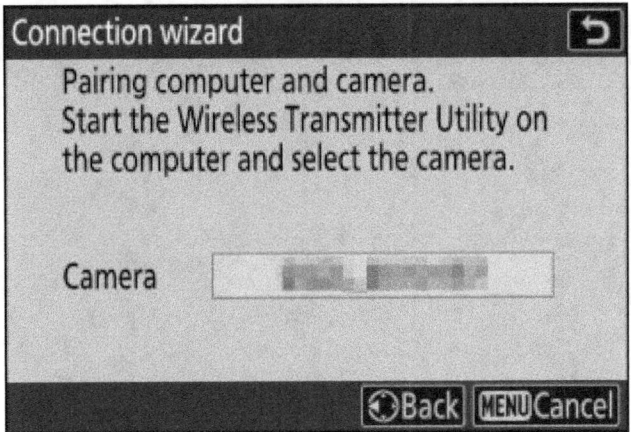

Start the computer's Wireless Transmitter Utility when requested to do so.

In Wireless Transmitter Software, choose the camera.

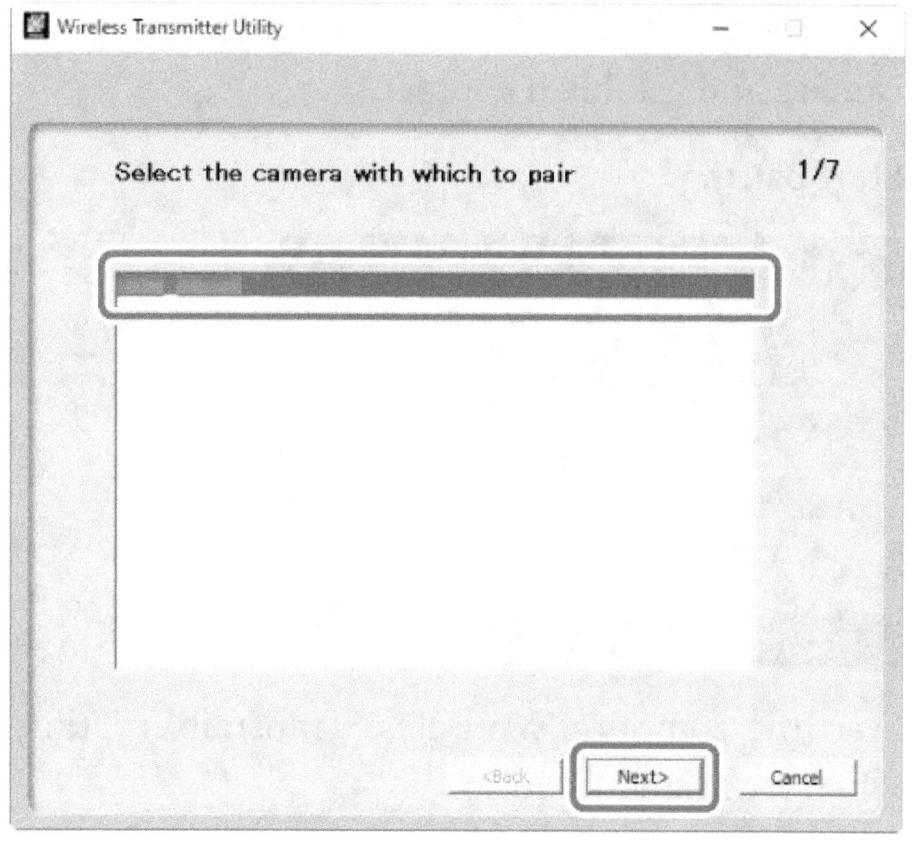

In Step 6, after reading the name presented by the camera, choose [Next].

Enter the camera's authentication code seen on-screen into the Wireless Transmitter Utility.

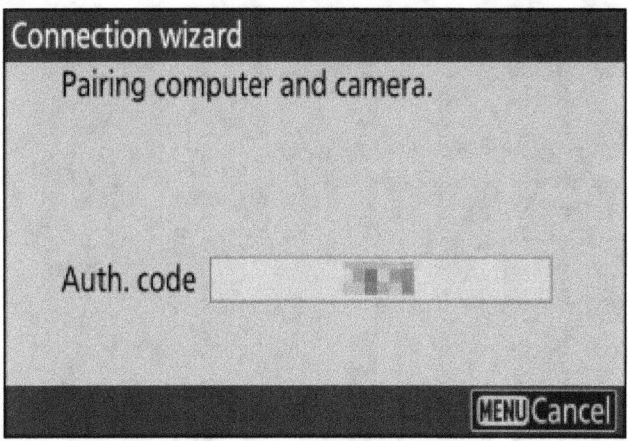

The camera will display a unique code that can only be used once.

Click [Next] when prompted to provide an authentication code in the Wireless Transmitter Utility.

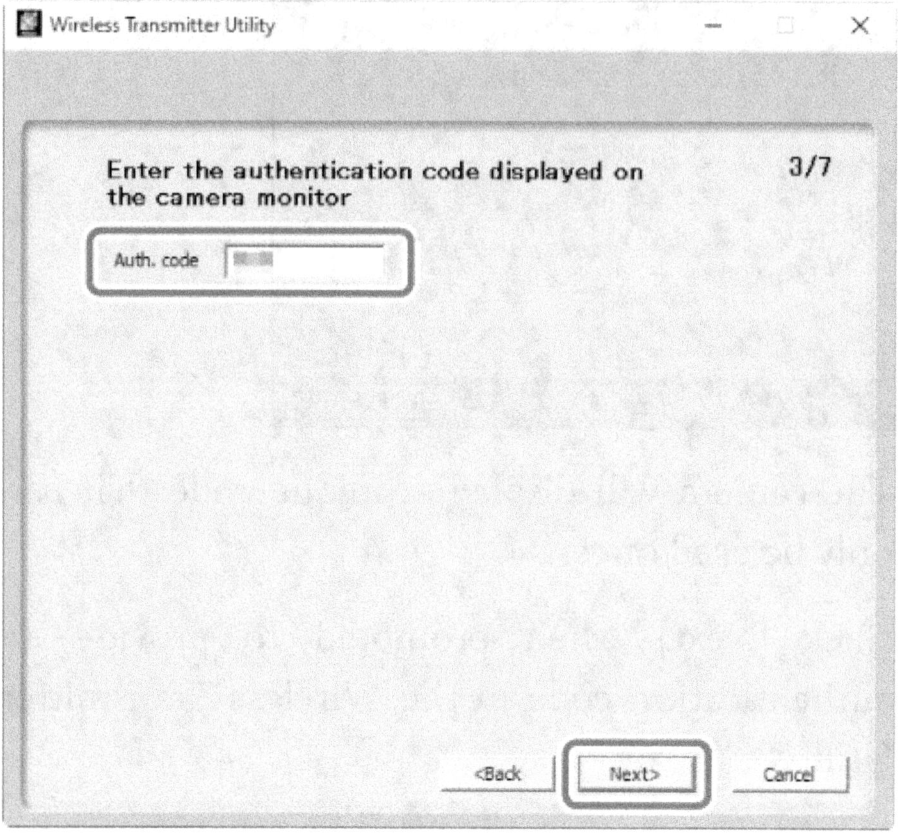

Finish the pairing.

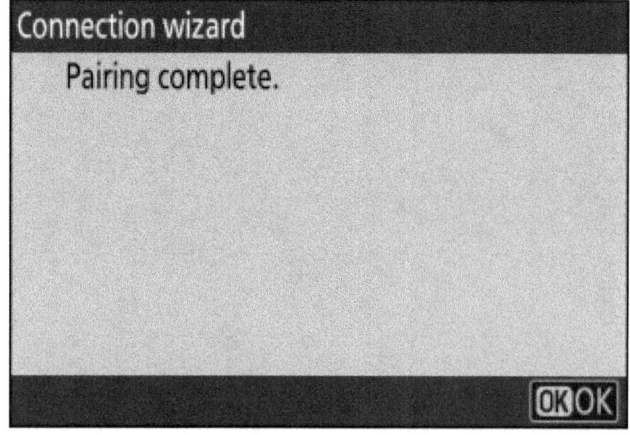

Press the J key when the camera confirms the pairing is complete.

When you choose [Next] in Wireless Transmitter Utility, you'll be requested to pick an output folder. Check out the Wireless Transmitter Utility's documentation page for further details.

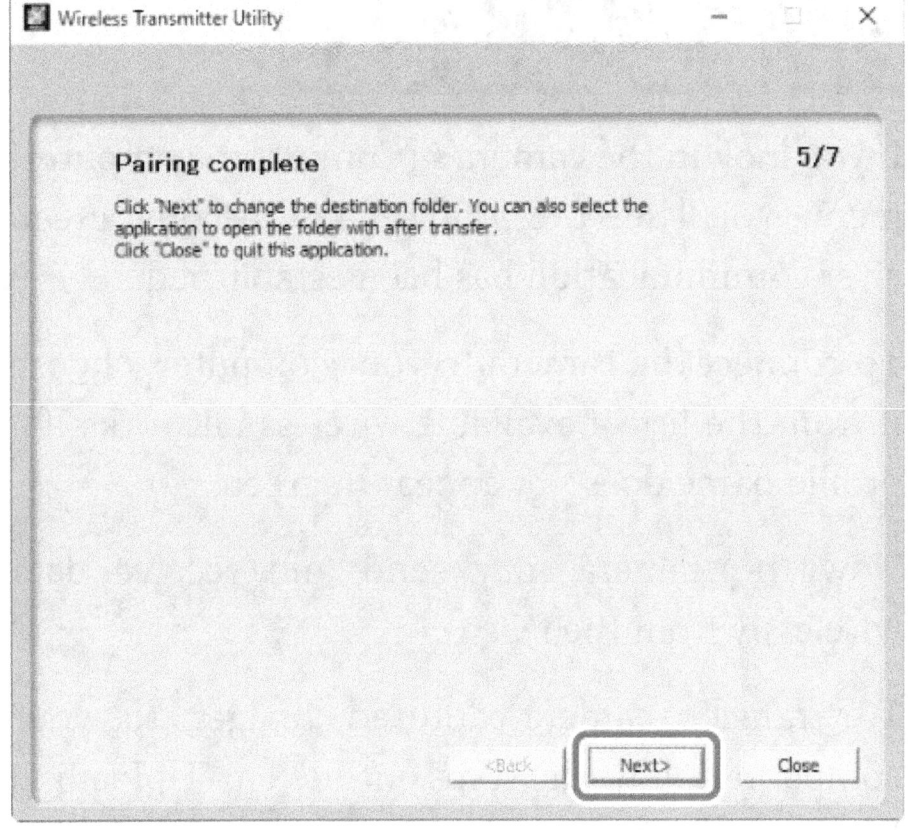

When paired successfully, your camera & computer will be able to communicate wirelessly.

Make sure everything is connected.

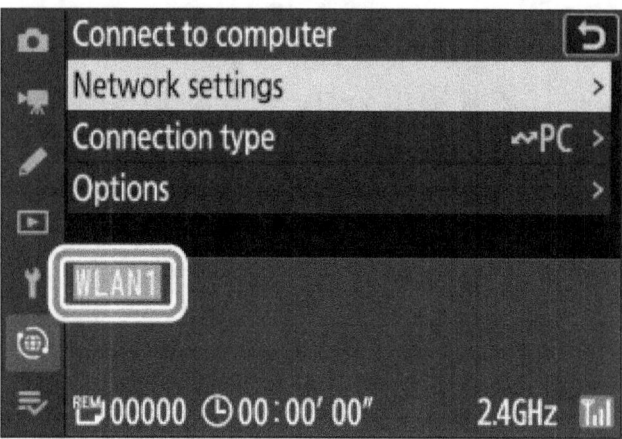

If you look in the camera's [Connect to computer] menu, you'll see the profile name become green after communication has been established.

To connect the camera to your computer, choose it from the list of available wireless networks if a profile name does not appear in green.

Now the camera may send and receive data wirelessly from the PC.

To transfer camera-captured images to your computer, follow the steps outlined in "Uploading Pictures" (Uploading Pictures).

Camera Control Pro 2 may be used to remotely operate a camera from a computer, and this guide will show you how to do just that (Camera Control).

Infrastructure-mode connectivity

Using a wireless router, the camera may be connected to any computer on existing network, even those in homes. In spite of the camera's presence, the computer may still access the web.

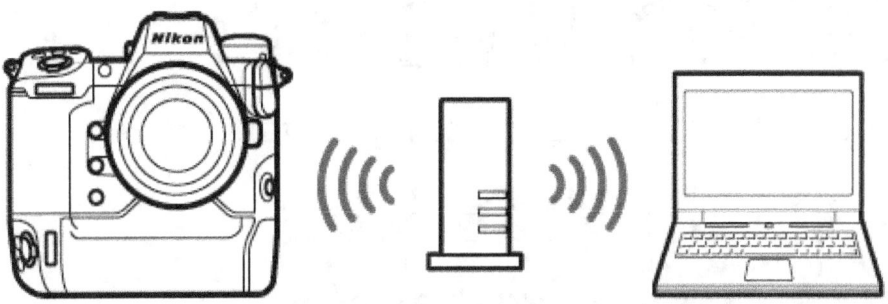

Make sure your Wireless Transmitter Utility is present on the PC before continuing.

Make sure the [Wired LAN] option is turned off in the network settings.

Infrastructure mode

In network menu, click "Connect to computer," then "Network settings," and finally "2.".

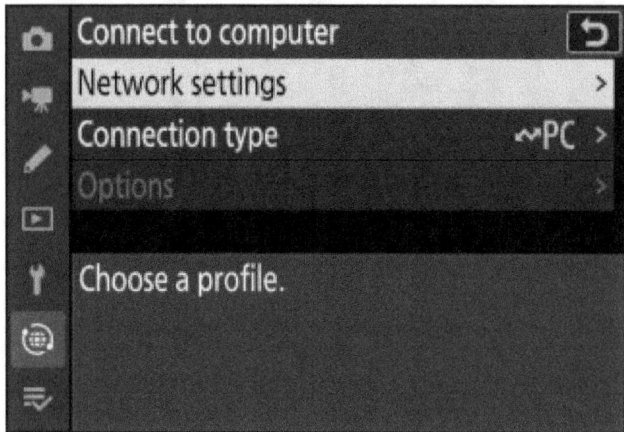

Highlight the [Create profile] the tap J.

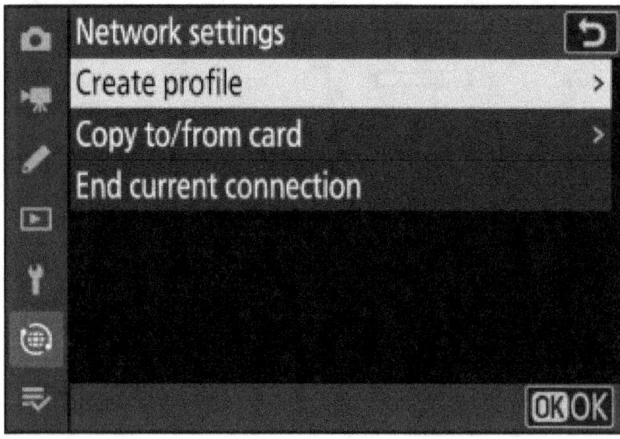

Title your new profile.

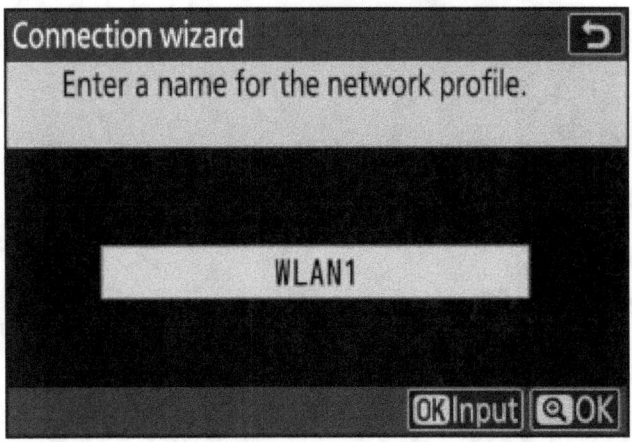

If you're OK with the default name and want to skip this stage, just hit the X.

Whatever you give your network connection will show up under [Connect to computer] > choose [Network settings] in the network menu.

Press J to rename the profile. Please refer to "Text Entry" for details on how to enter text (Text Entry). After a name is entered, press X to continue.

Select "Search Wi-fi" and hit "J".

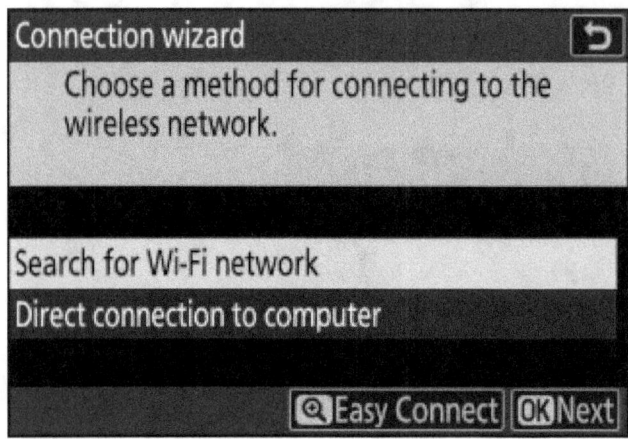

If there are any nearby networks, the camera will find them and label them (SSID).

Easy Connect

Select network.

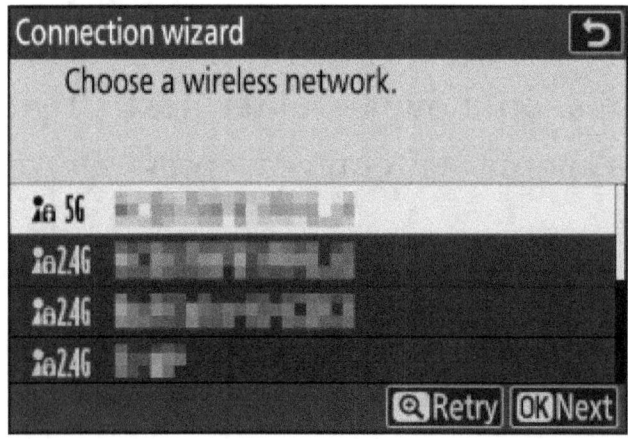

Select an SSID and hit the J key to join it.

Every SSID has a corresponding icon that depicts the frequency range across which it works.

To identify encrypted networks, look for the "h" symbol. If the network you've chosen requires encryption (h), you'll be requested to input the key. Step 7 should be performed if network is not encrypted

Press X to do a new search for the missing network.

Hidden SSIDs

Encryption key must be entered.

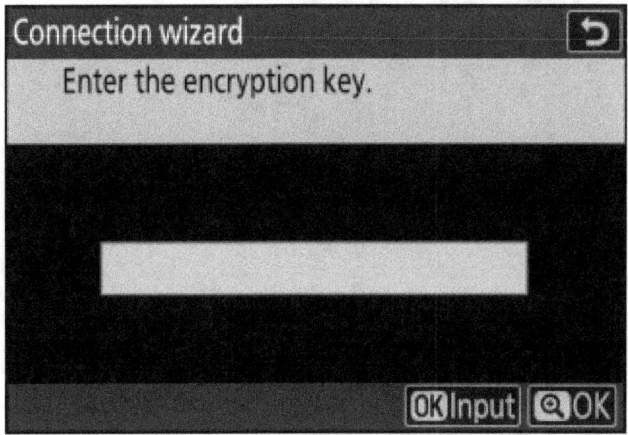

Touch J and type in wireless router encryption key

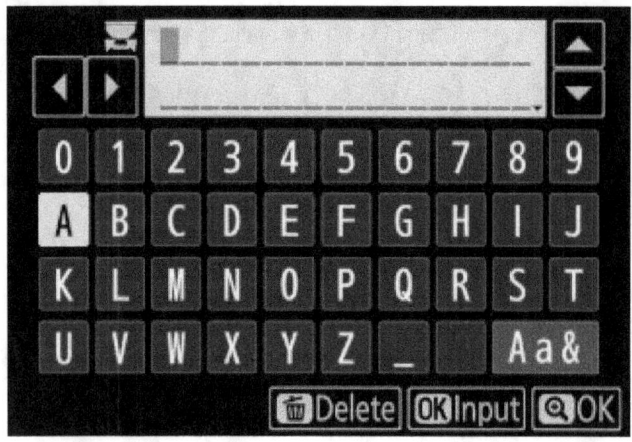

When finished, please press the X.

To continue the call, press X once more. When the link is successfully established, a brief message will appear on screen.

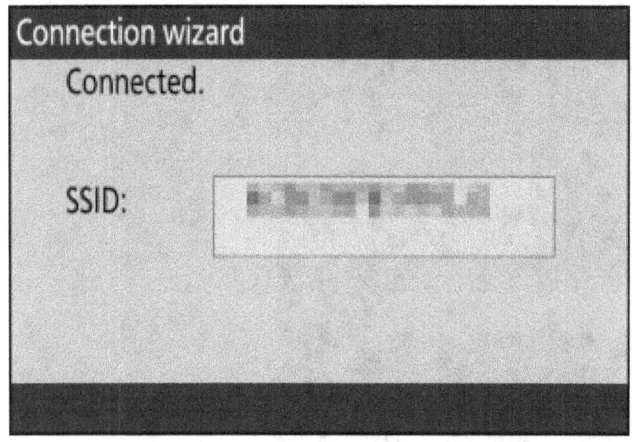

Select or get IP address.

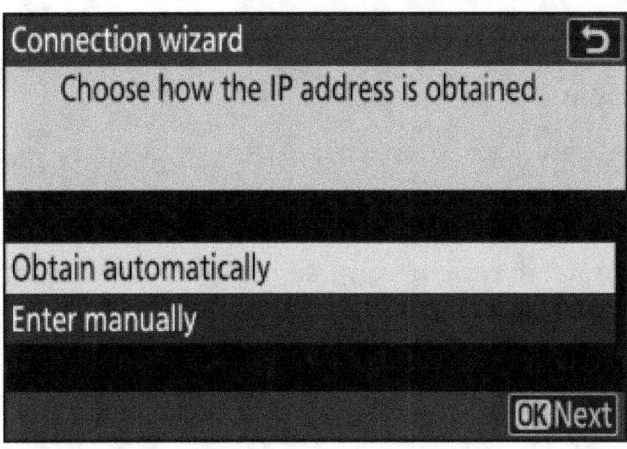

Choose any of these option and tap on J.

Option	Description
[Obtain automatically]	Select this option if the network is configured to supply the IP address automatically. A "configuration complete" message will be displayed once an IP address has been assigned.

[Enter manually]	Enter the IP address and sub-net mask manually. Press J; you will be prompted to enter the IP address. Rotate the main command dial to highlight segments. Press 4 or 2 to change the highlighted segment and press J to save changes. Next, press X; a "configuration complete" message will be displayed. Press X again to display the sub-net mask. Press 1 or 3 to edit the sub-net mask and press J; a "configuration complete" message will be displayed.

When the "configuration complete" message appears, press J to continue.

Start pairing.

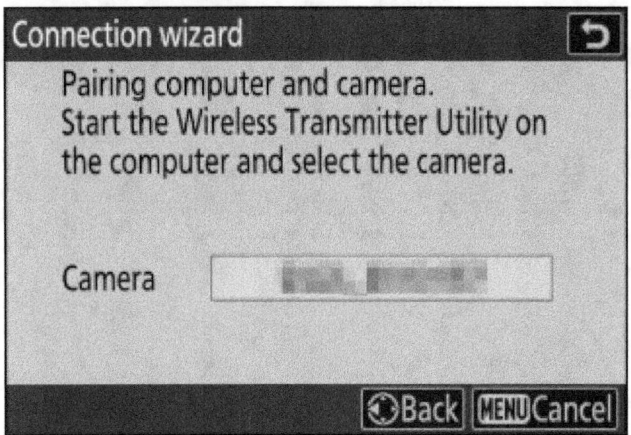

Start the computer's Wireless Transmitter Utility when requested to do so.

In Wireless Transmitter Software, choose the camera.

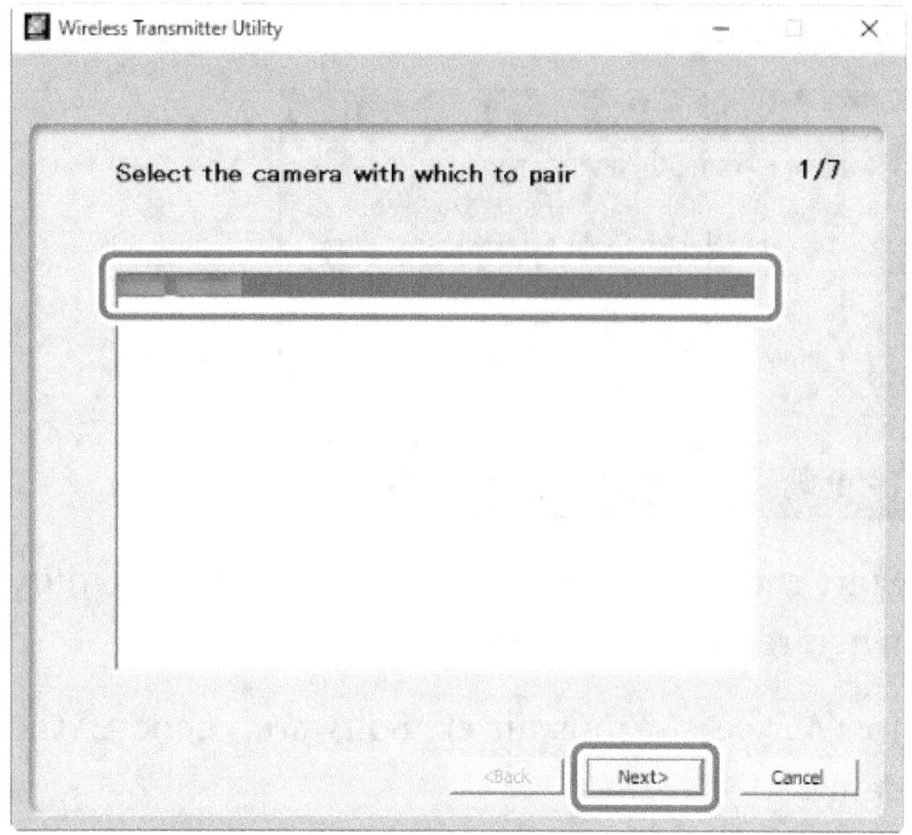

In Step 8, when the camera prompts you for a name, choose the one that appears.

Enter the camera's authentication code seen on-screen into the Wireless Transmitter Utility.

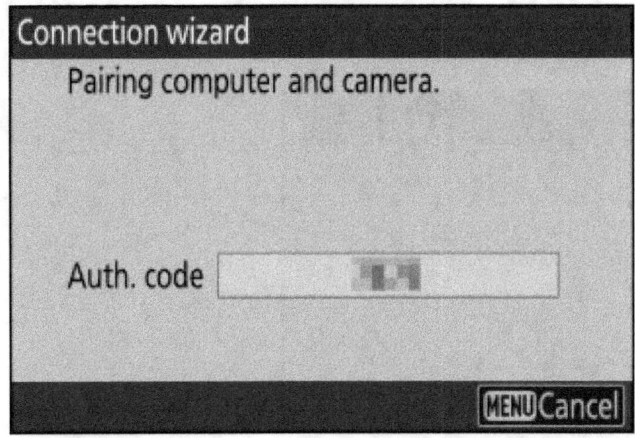

An authentication code will be shown on the camera. Using the Wireless Transmitter Utility's prompt, locate the authentication code and then click [Next].

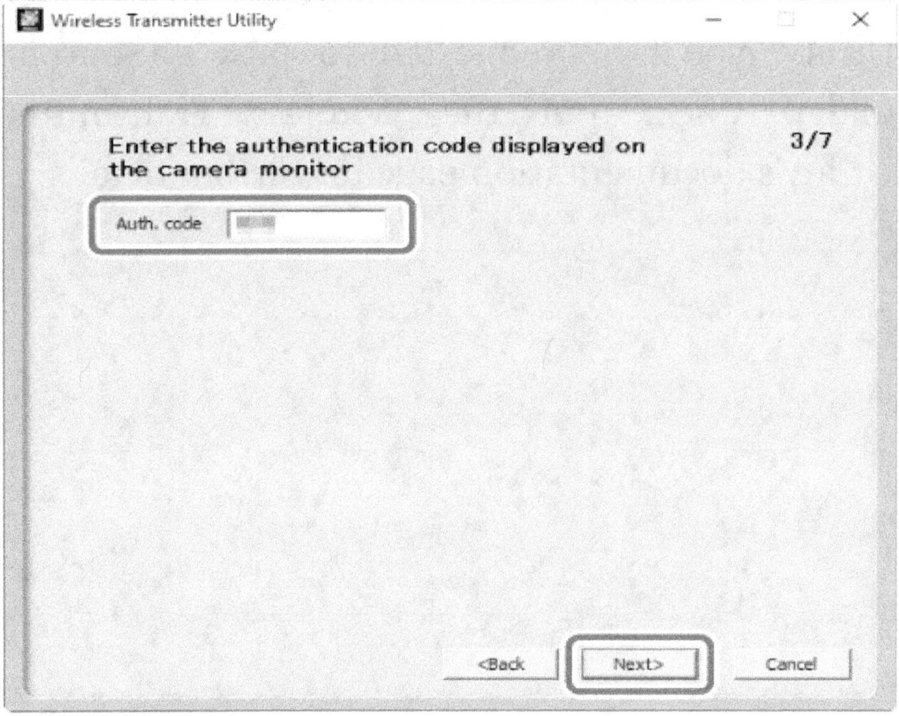

Complete pairing.

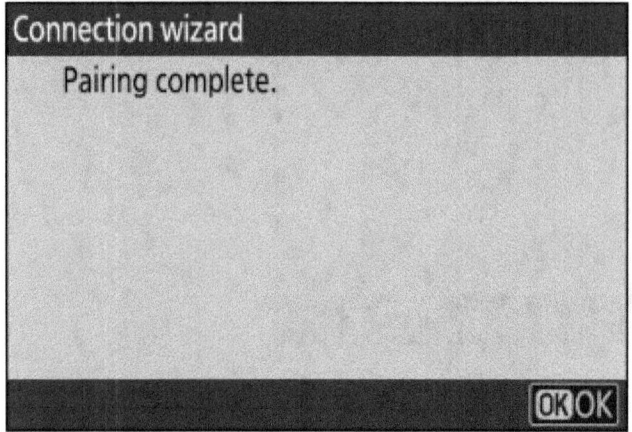

Press the J key when the camera confirms the pairing is complete.

When you choose [Next] in Wireless Transmitter Utility, you'll be requested to pick an output folder. Check out the Wireless Transmitter Utility's documentation page for further details.

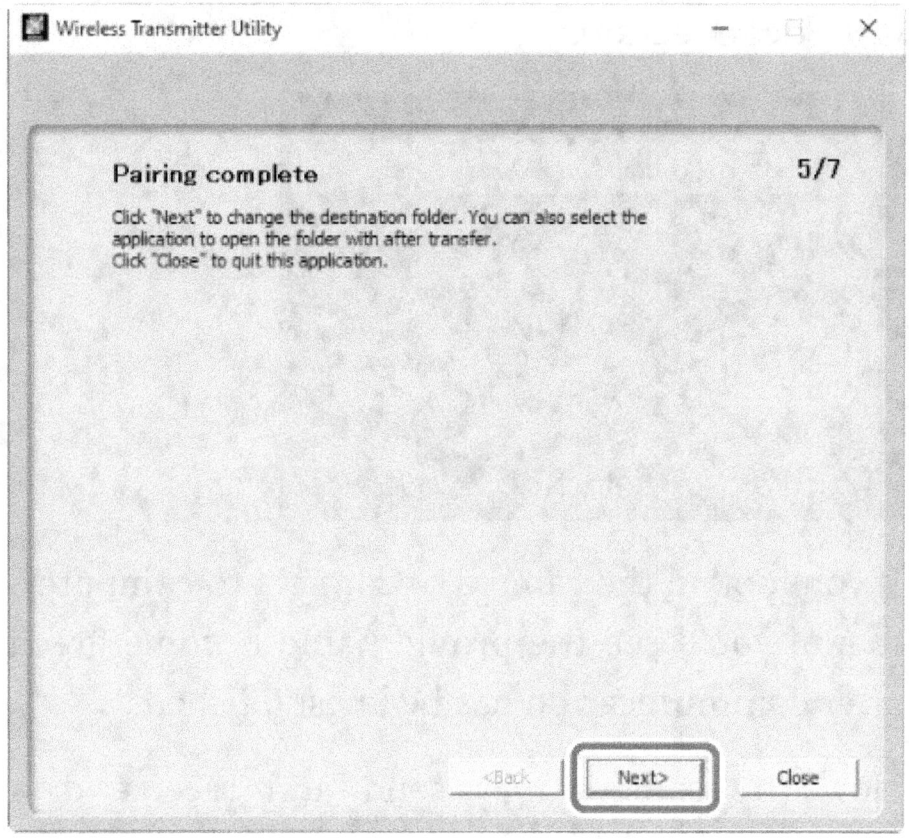

Once paired, the camera & computer will be able to communicate wirelessly.

Check connection.

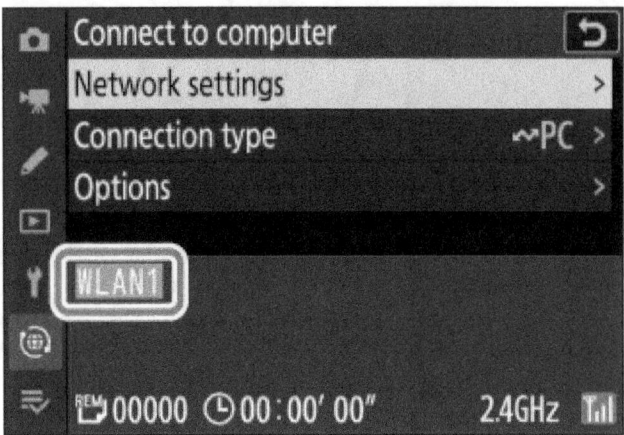

If you look in the camera's [Connect to computer] menu, you'll see the profile name become green after communication has been established.

Now the camera may send and receive data wirelessly from the PC.

To transfer camera-captured images to your computer, follow the steps outlined in "Uploading Pictures".

Camera Control Pro 2 may be used to remotely operate a camera from a computer, and this guide will show you how to do just that (Camera Control).

Ethernet Connection

Through its Ethernet port, the camera may be connected to computers directly or to preexisting networks.

Connect Ethernet Cable

The camera should be linked to a network through an Ethernet connection. Connectors should not be pushed in or inserted at an angle. You'll need to plug the other end of the cord into a device like a computer or a router.

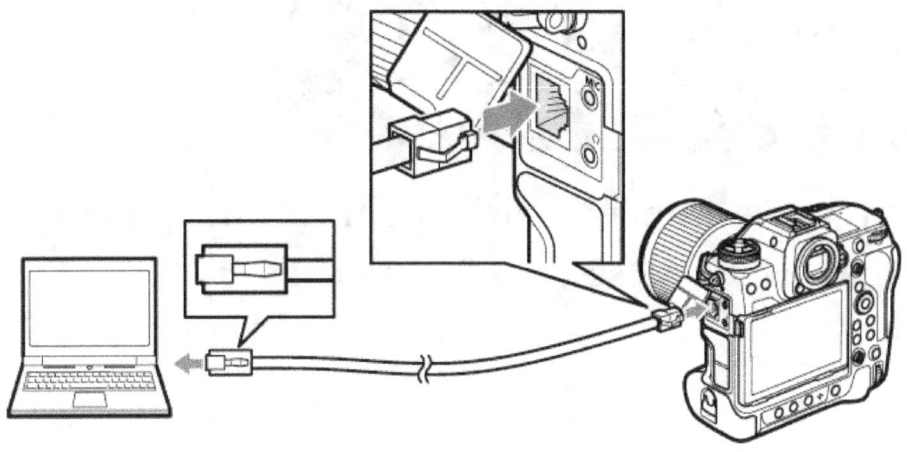

Profiles in Ethernet Network

Make sure an Ethernet wire is connected to your camera and Wireless Transmitter Utility is running on the PC before continuing.

To activate [Wired LAN] under the network settings, set the toggle to [ON].

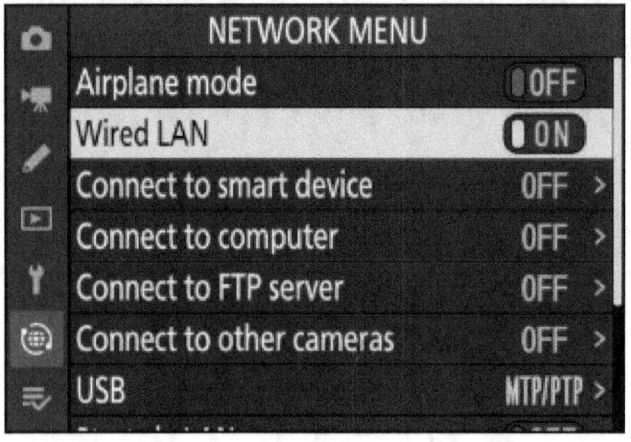

In network menu, click "Connect to computer," then "Network settings," and finally "2."

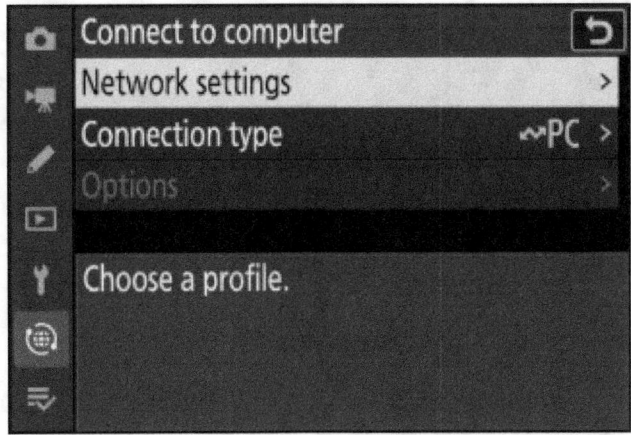

Select [Create profile] then touch J.

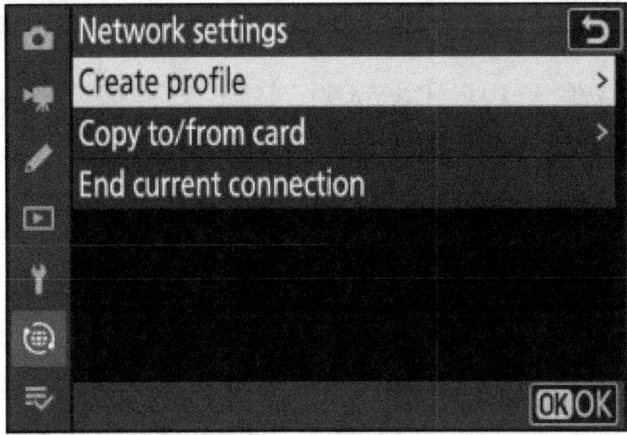

Title your new profile.

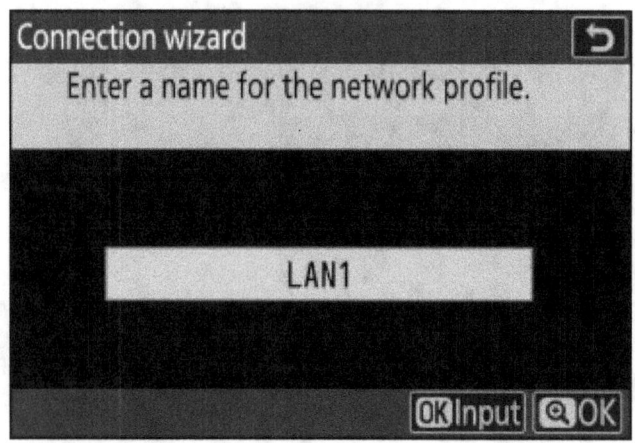

If you're OK with the default name and want to skip this stage, just hit the X.

Whatever you give your network connection will show up under [Connect computer] > select [Network settings] in the network menu.

Press J to rename the profile. Please refer to "Text Entry" for details on how to enter text (Text Entry). After a name is entered, press X to continue.

It's necessary to get an IP address, which you may either choose or be assigned.

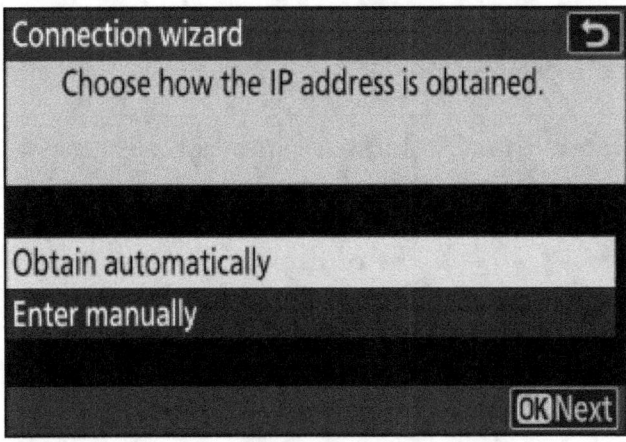

Select any of the below options and touch J.

Option	Description
[Obtain automatically]	Select this option if the network is configured to supply the IP address automatically. A "configuration complete" message will be displayed once an IP address has been assigned.

Option	Description
[Enter manually]	Enter the IP address and sub-net mask manually.

Press J; you will be prompted to enter the IP address.

Rotate the main command dial to highlight segments.

Press 4 or 2 to change the highlighted segment and press J to save changes.

Next, press X; a "configuration complete" message will be displayed. Press X again to display the sub-net mask.

Press 1 or 3 to edit the sub-net mask and press J; a "configuration complete" message will be displayed. |

Touch J to continue after a completed

Start pairing.

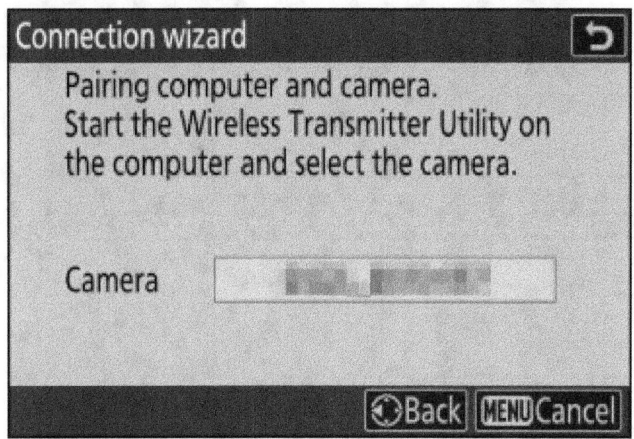

Start the computer's Wireless Transmitter Utility when requested to do so.

In Wireless Transmitter Software, choose the camera.

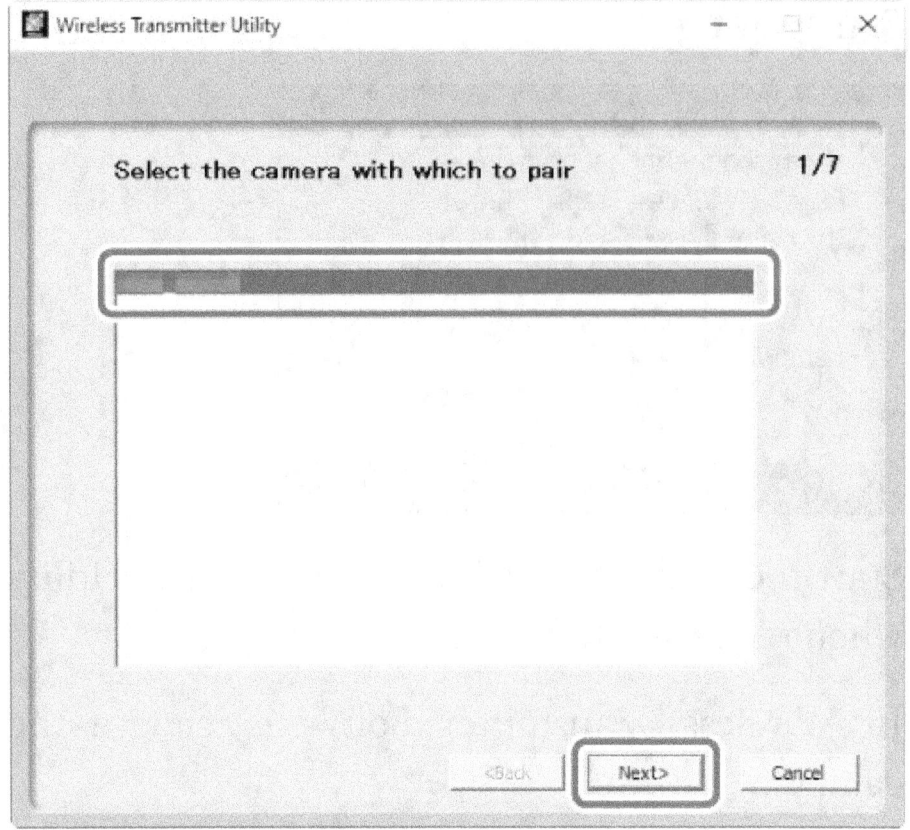

In Step 6, after reading the name presented by the camera, choose [Next].

Enter the camera's authentication code seen on-screen into the Wireless Transmitter Utility.

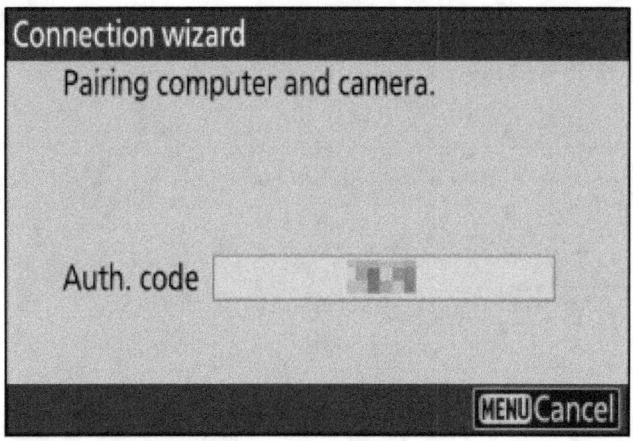

An authentication code will be shown on the camera.

Wireless Transmitter Utility will prompt you for an authentication code; enter it here and click [Next].

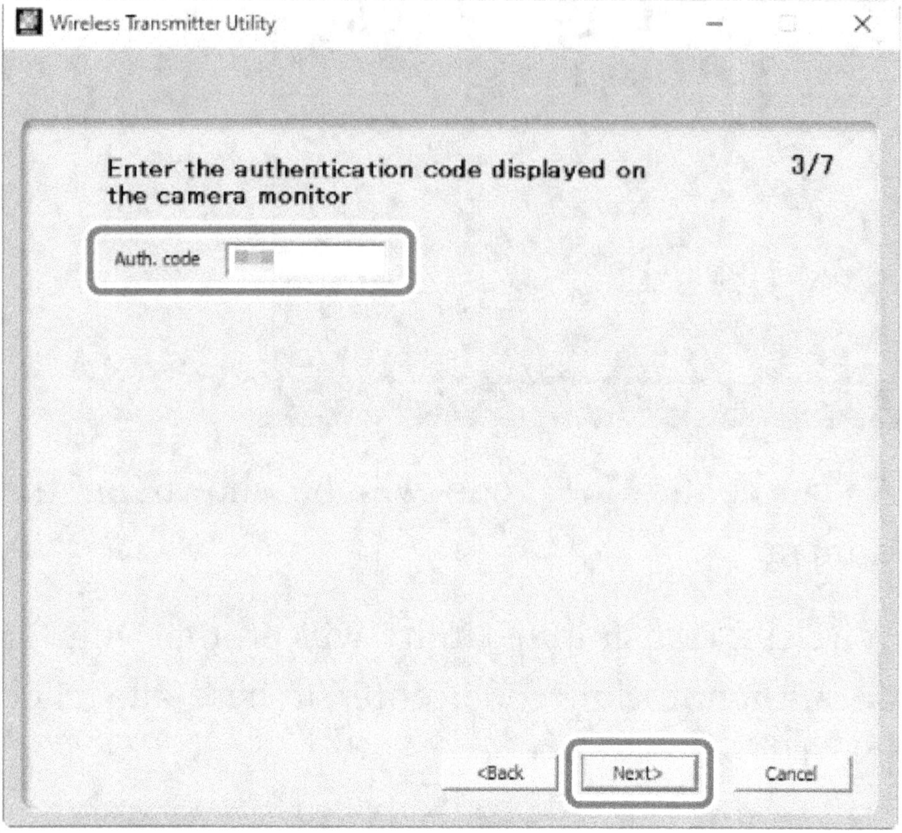

Complete pairing.

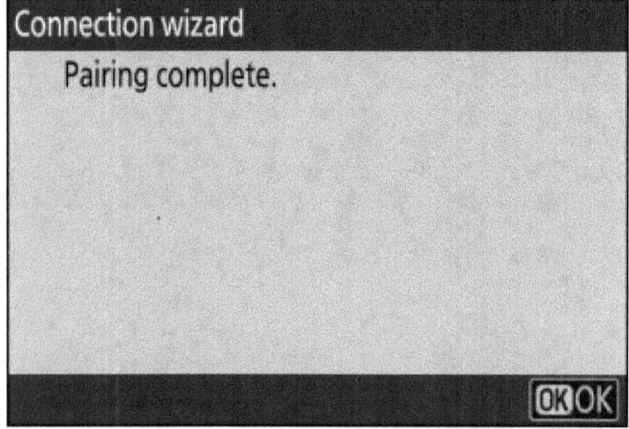

Press the J key when the camera confirms the pairing is complete.

When you choose [Next] in Wireless Transmitter Utility, you'll be requested to pick an output folder. Check out the Wireless Transmitter Utility's documentation page for further details.

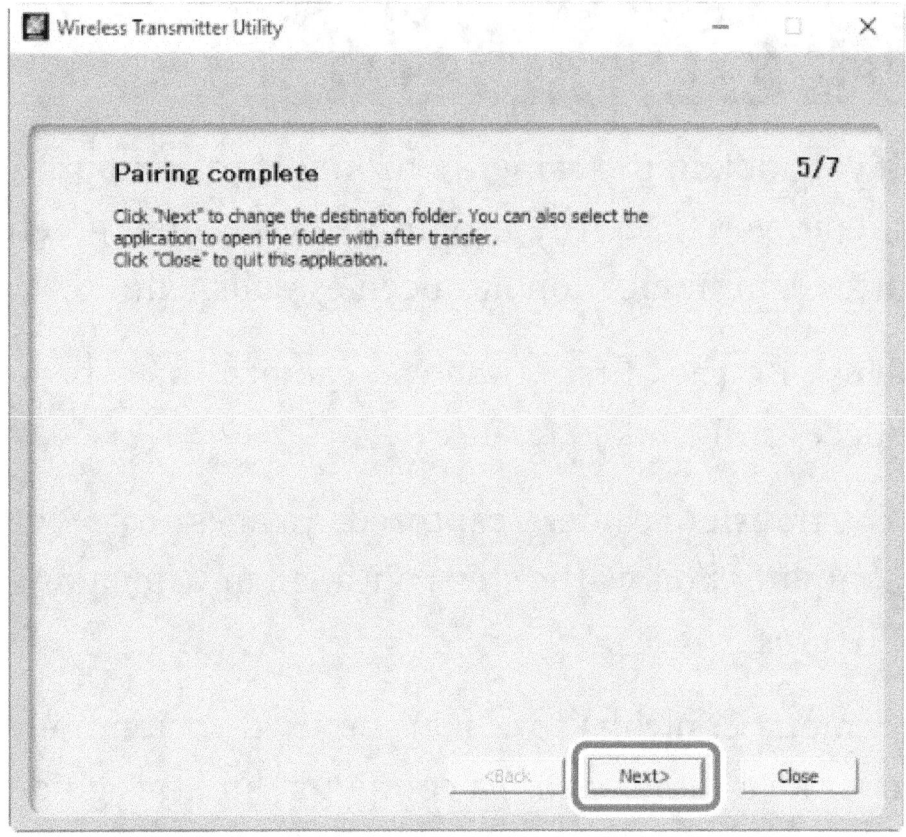

After successful pairing, a link will be created between camera and the computer.

Make sure everything is connected.

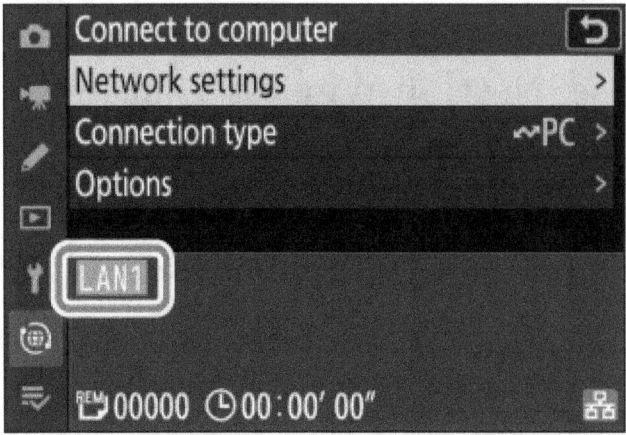

If you look in the camera's [Connect to computer] menu, you'll see the profile name become green after communication has been established.

This is the first time a camera has been successfully linked to a PC.

To transfer camera-captured images to your computer, follow the steps outlined in "Uploading Pictures".

Camera Control Pro 2 may be used to remotely operate a camera from a computer, and this guide will show you how to do just that (Camera Control).

Uploading Pictures

During the playing process, you may choose which images to submit. They may also be posted automatically as they're taken.

Make sure your camera is linked to your computer through Ethernet or wireless network before attempting to upload any photos. Join using a predefined host profile chosen from the [Connect computer] >select [Network settings] menu.

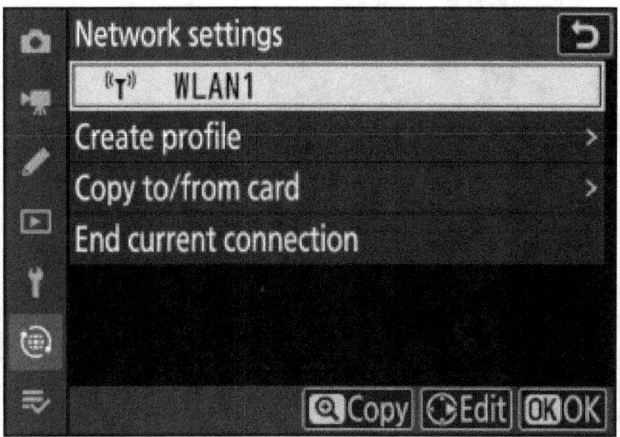

Whenever a connection has been established, its profile name will be shown in green in camera.

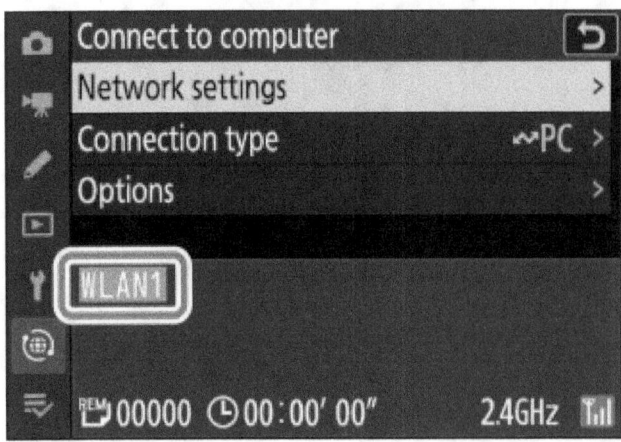

Select your Pictures for the Upload

In [Connect to computer], choose [Picture transfer] > Select [Connection Type] from the Network Settings Menu.

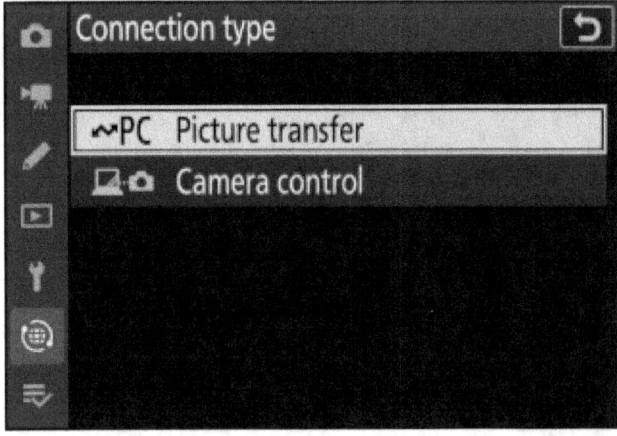

Choose full-frame or choose thumbnail playback by pressing the K button on the camera.

To get more information about a photo, select it and then hit the *i* button.

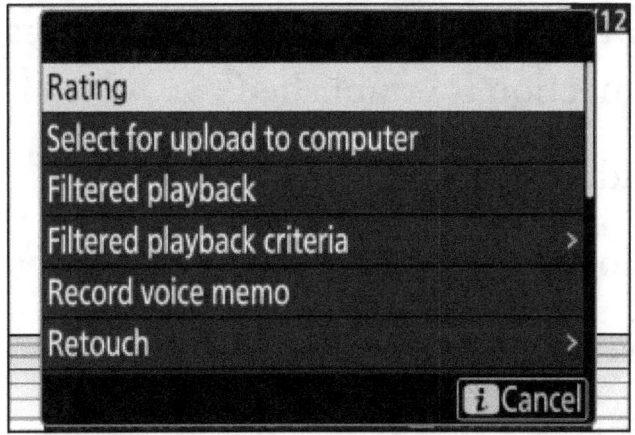

Choose [Select for uploads to a computer] then touch J.

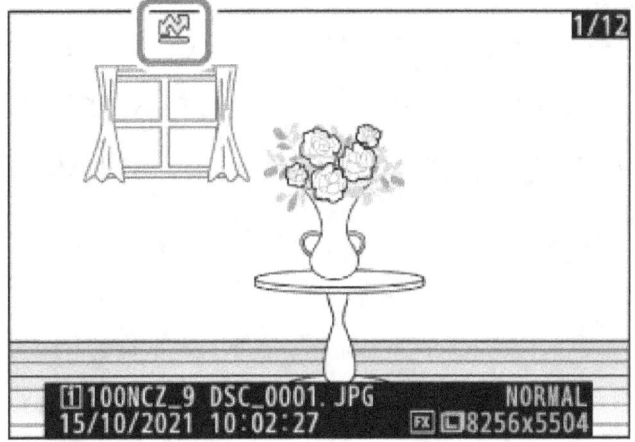

This will be shown by a white "priority upload" symbol on the image. When a camera is online, the upload indicator becomes green to indicate that the process may begin.

In any other case, the upload process will begin as soon as the connection is established.

If you want to add more photos, just do it again.

Unmarking Upload

Filtering Images Before Uploading

Real-time image uploading

If you have [ON] selected for [Connect to computer] > you may immediately upload photographs as they are taken. For more customization, please visit our [Options] > Network settings may be automated using a [Auto upload] option.

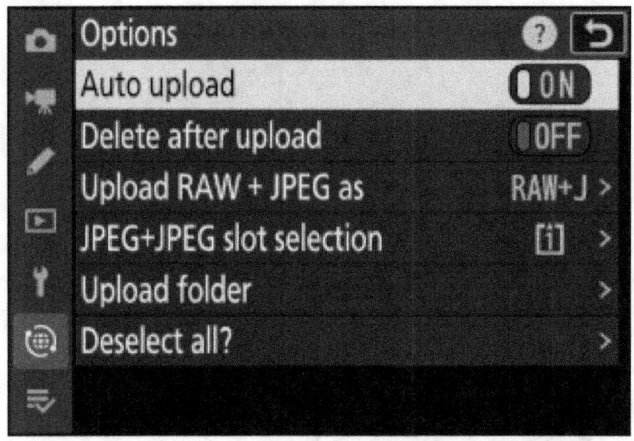

Once the image has been saved on the memory card, the upload process may begin. Remember to load up the camera with a fresh memory card before you start shooting.

The uploading of videos does not occur automatically. Instead, they must be manually uploaded through the playback screen.

Upload Icon

It indicates the uploading status.

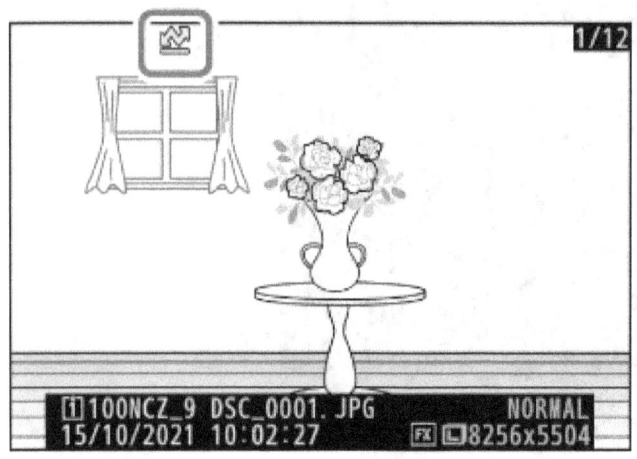

s (white): a priority upload

This photo was chosen for uploading by hand. Photos with this symbol will be posted before those with the W ("upload") icon.

W (white): Upload

However, the upload hasn't yet commenced despite the photo being chosen.

X (green): Uploading

in progress.

Y (blue): Uploaded

Completed upload

[Connect to the Computer] Status will be Display

It will show the below:

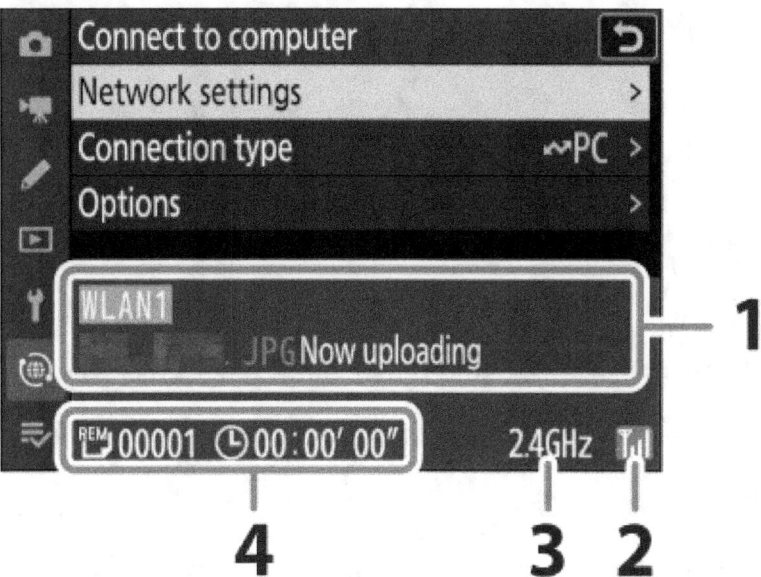

1. Status: The status of the connection to the host. The profile name is displayed in green when a connection is established.

    While files are being transferred, the status display shows "Now uploading" preceded by the name of the file being sent. Errors are also displayed here.

2. Signal strength: Ethernet connections are shown by d. When the camera is connected to a wireless network, the icon instead shows the wireless signal strength.

3	Band: The band used by the wireless network to which the camera is connected in infrastructure mode.
4	Pictures/time remaining: The number of pictures remaining and the time needed to send them. The time remaining is an estimate only.

Camera Control

If you have Camera Ctrl Pro 2 installed on your computer, you may use it to operate the camera. You can snap pictures with no memory card in the camera since they may be stored on the computer instead.

When making movies, a memory card is still required.

When in camera control mode, the camera's standby timer will not run out.

In order to use Camera Ctrl Pro 2, you must first establish a connection between your camera and computer using either an Ethernet cable or a wireless network. Connect using a predefined host profile chosen from the [Connect to the computer] > [Network settings] menu.

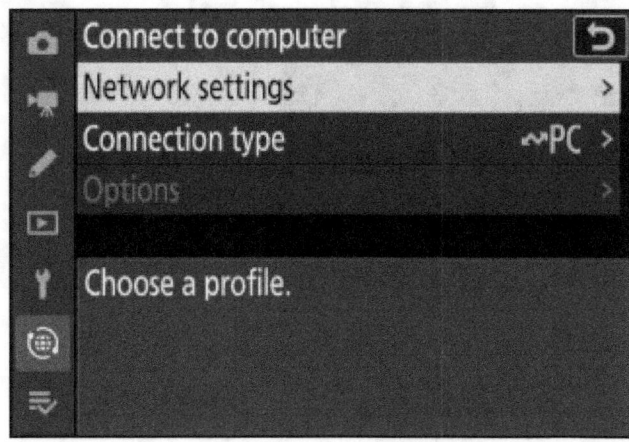

When successfully linked, the camera's [Connect to computer] option will show the profile's name in green.

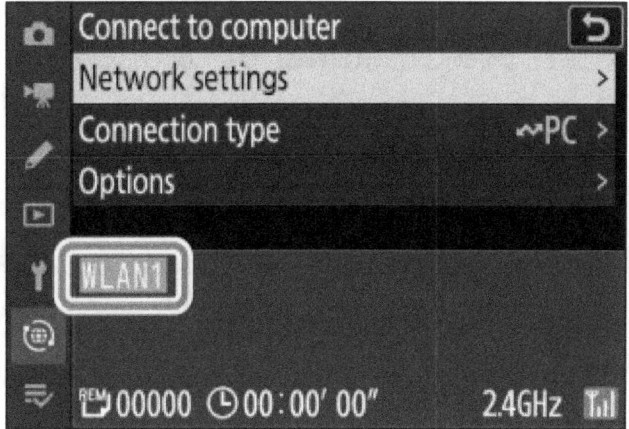

Choose "Camera control" > Connect to the computer" > The [Connection Type] option under Network Settings.

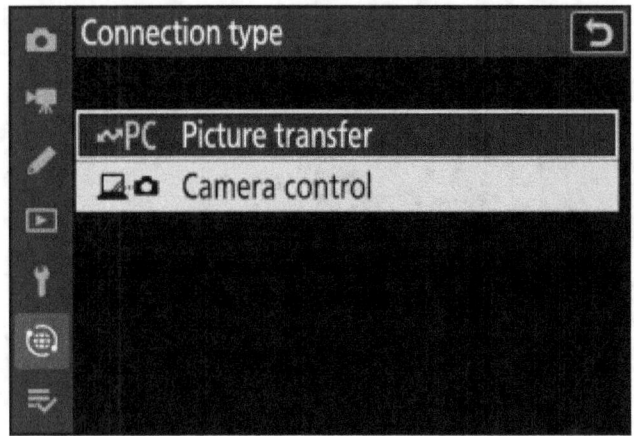

To use Camera Control Pro 2, start up the instance on the host machine.

Control the camera with Camera Ctrl Pro 2.

See the Camera Ctrl Pro 2 manual or online help for details on how to take images using the program.

[Connect to the Computer] Cam Control Screen

Shows the below:

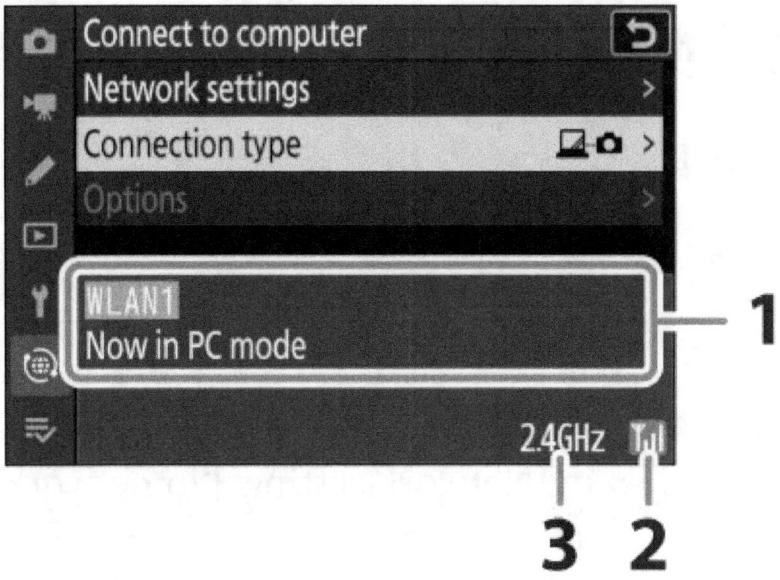

1	Status: The status of the connection to the host. The profile name is displayed in green when a connection is established. Errors are also displayed here (Troubleshooting Wireless LAN and Ethernet Connections).
2	Signal strength: Ethernet connections are shown by d. When the camera is connected to a wireless network, the icon instead shows the wireless signal strength.
3	Band: The band used by the wireless network to which the camera is connected in infrastructure mode.

End your Camera and computer Connection

End your connection by:

Turn your camera off.

Select [End the current connection] in [Connect to the computer] > in [Network settings] in network menu, or

You connect to smart device using Bluetooth or Wi-Fi.

FTP Servers: Connecting through Ethernet or through Wireless LAN

The camera's Wi-Fi (wireless LAN) functionality or an external Ethernet cable plugged into the camera's Ethernet connection allow it to connect to the FTP servers & upload images across preexisting networks. There is also direct FTP server connection support for the camera.

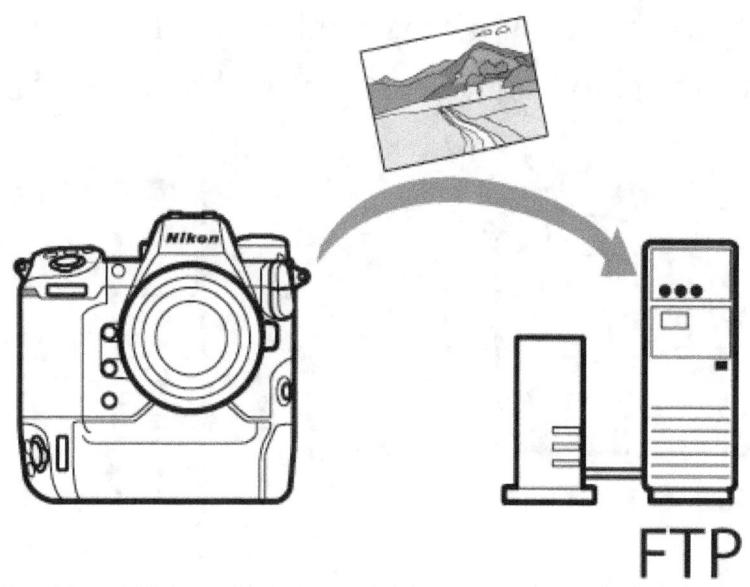

Wireless LAN

The camera may contact FTP servers through a direct wireless connection (access-point mode) or through a wireless router on an already-established network, such as home networks (under infrastructure mode).

Direct Wireless Connect (Access-Point)

There is a direct wireless connection between the camera and the FTP server. The camera may be used as wireless LAN access point, allowing you to connect to the network even when your computer is not in range of a wireless router or access point.

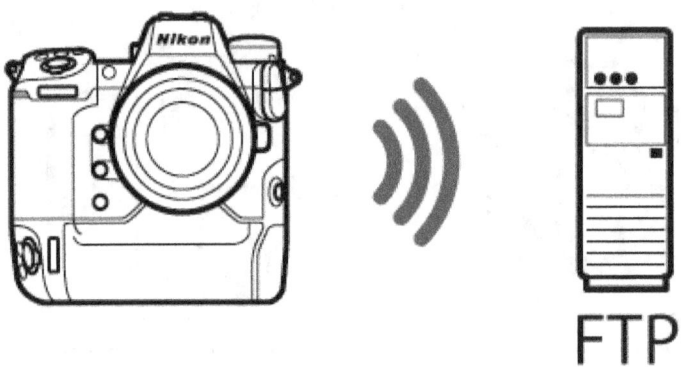

Create host profile with cam-connection wizard

Make sure the [Wired LAN] option is turned off in the network settings.

In the network menu, choose "Connect to FTP server," then select "Network settings" and hit "2."

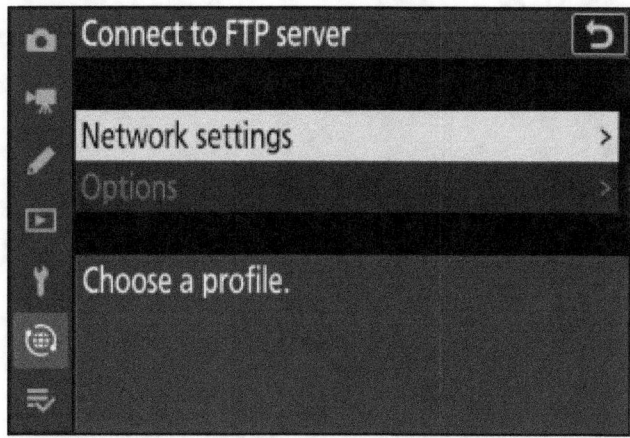

Select [Create profile] then touch on J.

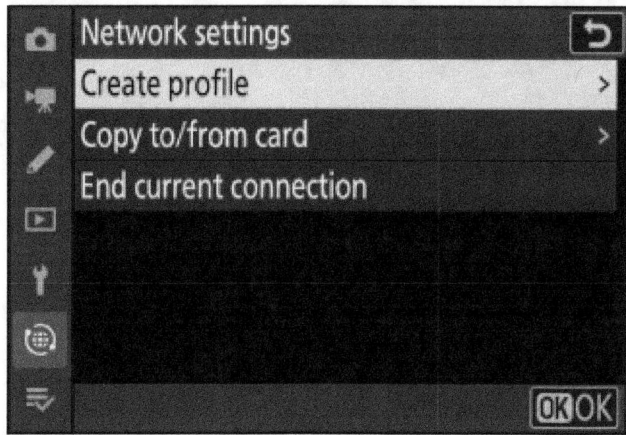

Select [Connection wizard] then touch 2.

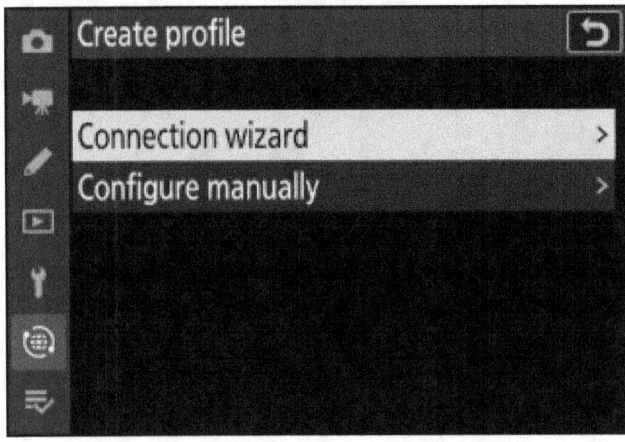

Connection wizard is launched.

Manual Configuration

Title the fresh profile.

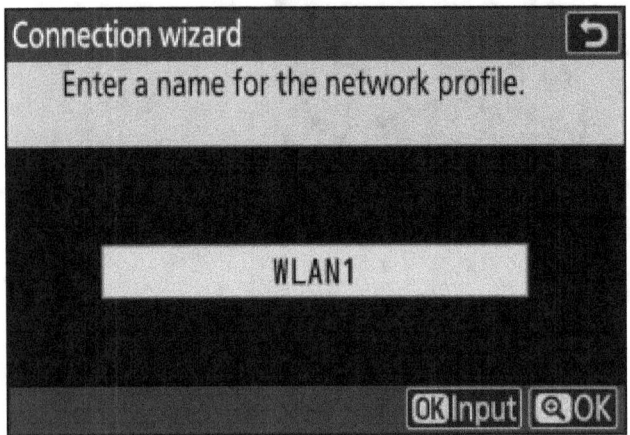

If you're OK with the default name and want to skip this stage, just hit the X.

What you call it will show up in the [Connect with FTP server] > in [Network settings] choice in the network menu.

Press J to rename the profile. Please refer to "Text Entry" for details on how to enter text (Text Entry). After a name is entered, press X to continue.

Select "Direct computer connection" and hit the J key.

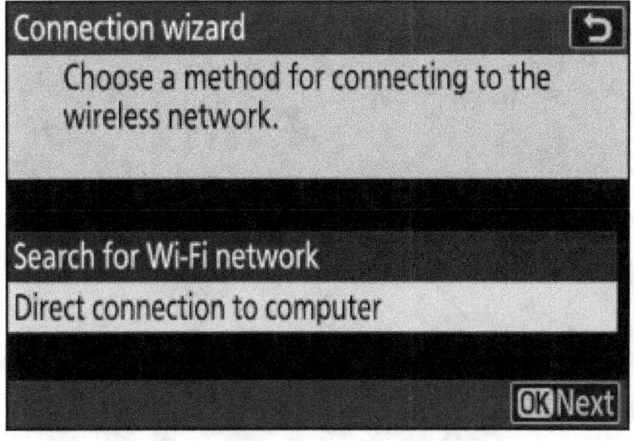

Your cam SSID & encryption key is displayed.

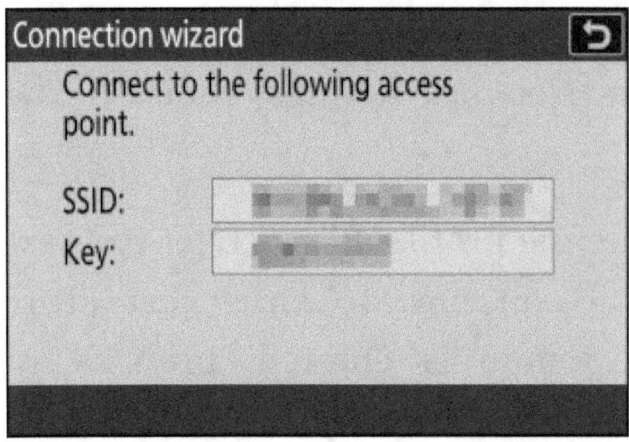

Create connection to your camera.

Windows:

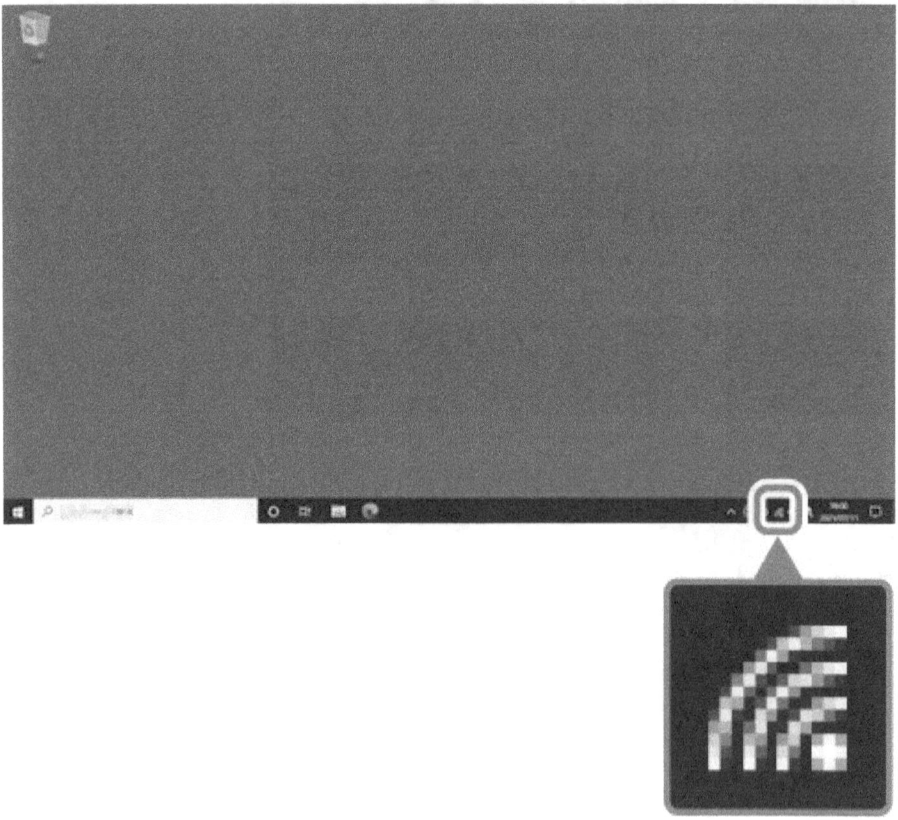

To access a wireless network, tap the corresponding icon in the system tray.

Step 5: Click the camera's SSID shown on your device.

In Step 5, the camera will show an encryption key; use this to input network security key when requested. The computer will reach out to the camera and establish contact.

macOS:

To activate wireless LAN, choose the corresponding menu item.

Step 5: Click the camera's SSID shown on your device.

In Step 5, the camera will show an encryption key; use this to input network security key when requested. The camera will connect to the PC after being asked to do so.

Select the kind of server.

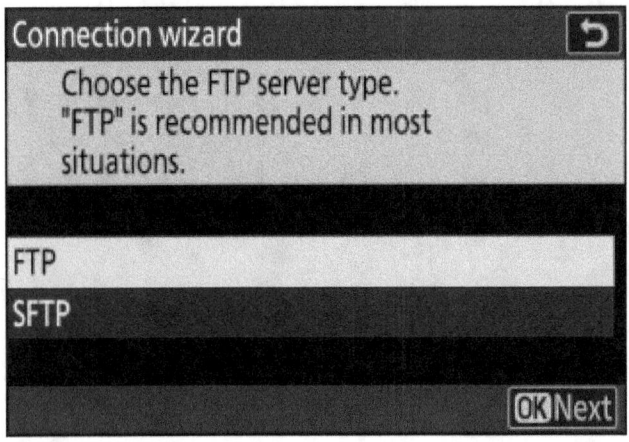

In order to choose a login method, select [FTP] or select [SFTP] (secure FTP) then touch J.

Log in.

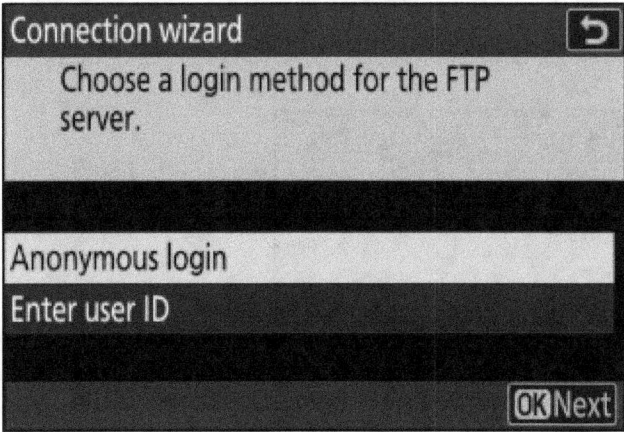

Select any of the below and touch J.

Option	Description
[Anonymous login]	Select this option if the server does not require a user ID or password. This option can only be used with servers that are configured for anonymous login. If login is successful, the camera will prompt you to choose a destination.
[Enter user ID]	Enter a user ID and password. Press J to log in when entry is complete. If login is successful, the camera will prompt you to choose a destination.

Firewall Settings

Select destination folder.

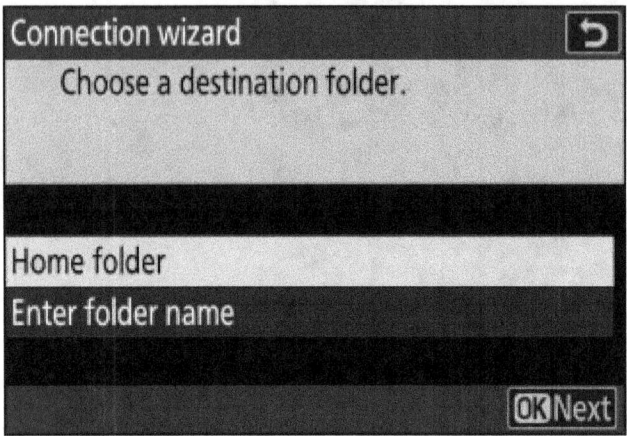

Select any of the below and touch J.

Option	Description
[Home folder]	Select this option to select the server's home folder as the destination for pictures uploaded from the camera. A "setup complete" dialog will be displayed if the operation is successful.
[Enter folder name]	Enter the destination folder name manually. The folder must already exist on the server. Enter the folder name and path when prompted and press J to display the "setup complete" dialog.

Check connection.

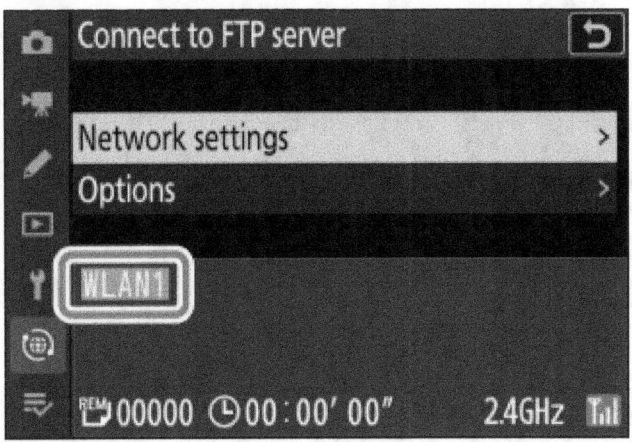

Once connected, the camera's [Connect with FTP server] option will show the profile's name in green.

If the camera's profile name isn't green, try connecting to it using the FTP server's wireless network list.

The camera and FTP server may now communicate with one another wirelessly.

After taking a picture using the camera, you may transfer it to your computer over FTP as explained in "Uploading Pictures" (Uploading Pictures).

Connect in Infrastructure Mode

Through a wireless router, the camera may connect to FTP server on already-established network, such as a home network.

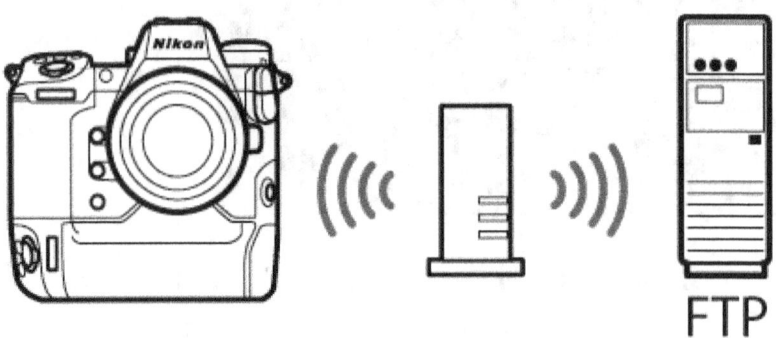

You may use camera connection wizard to set up a host profile.

Make sure that [Wired LAN] is turned off in the network settings before establishing a wireless connection.

Infrastructure mode

In the network menu, choose "Connect to FTP server," then select "Network settings" and hit "2.".

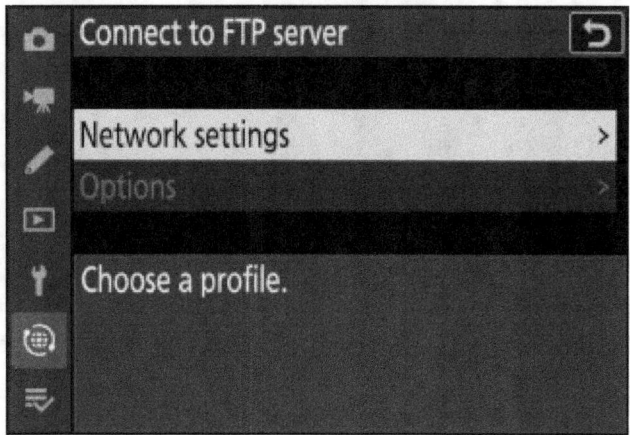

Select [Create profile] then touch J.

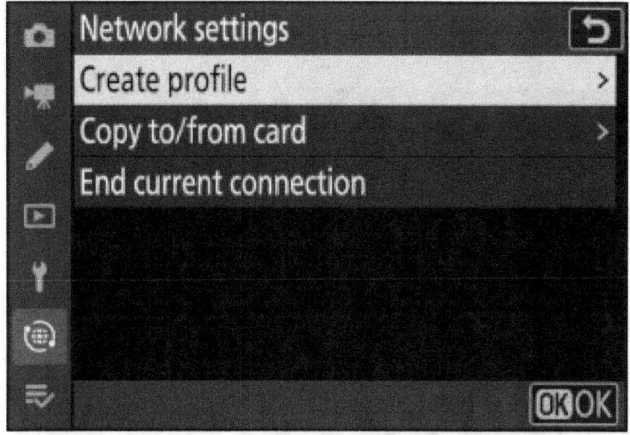

Select [Connection wizard] then touch 2.

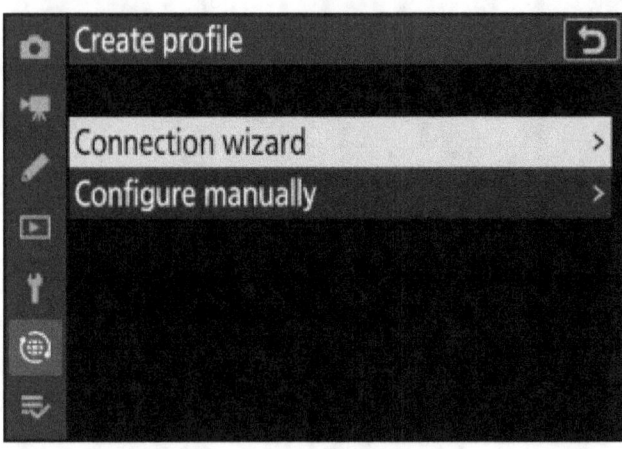

Launches connection wizard

Title the fresh profile.

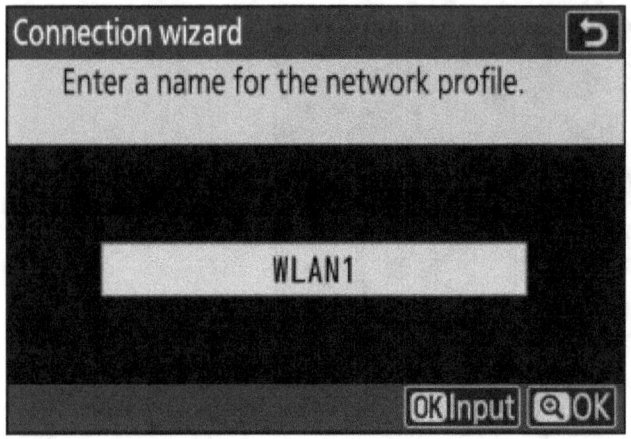

If you're OK with the default name and want to skip this stage, just hit the X.

What you call it will show up in the [Connect with FTP server] > in [Network settings] choice in the network menu.

Press J to rename the profile. Please refer to "Text Entry" for details on how to enter text (Text Entry). After a name is entered, press X to continue.

Select "Search for the wireless networks" and hit "J".

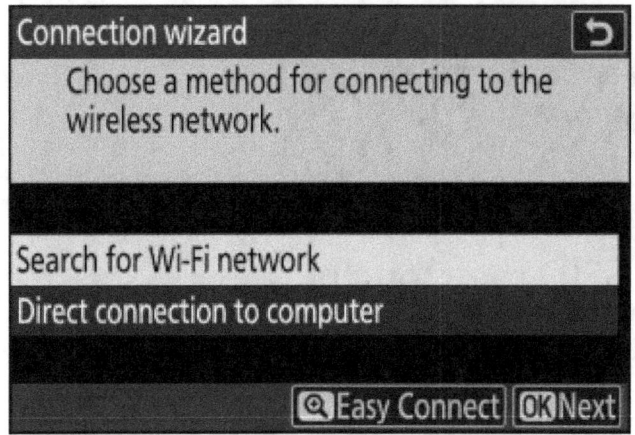

If there are any nearby networks, the camera will find them and label them (SSID).

Easy Connect

Select network.

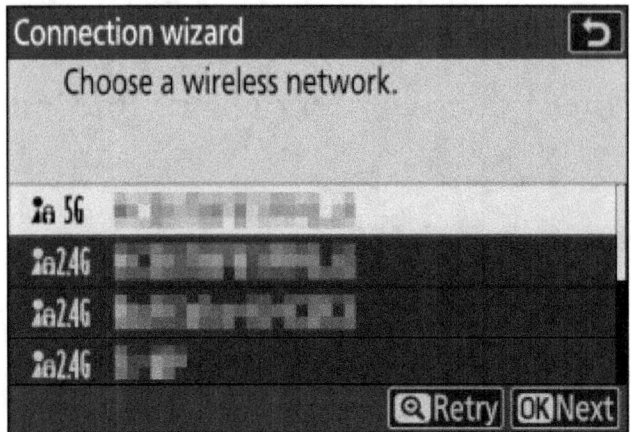

Select network SSID then touch J.

Every SSID has a corresponding icon that depicts the frequency range across which it works.

To identify encrypted networks, look for the "h" symbol. If the network you've chosen requires encryption (h), you'll be requested to input the key. Step 8 is used when network is not encrypted.

If the network you want isn't listed, hit X to start again.

Hidden SSIDs

Type in encryption key.

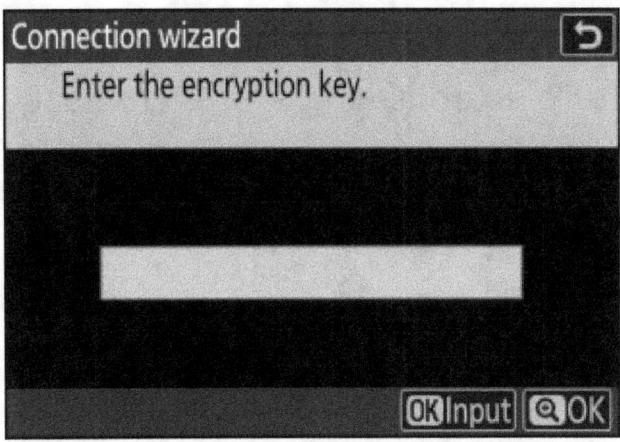

To access the wireless router's secure configuration menu, please press J and input the encryption key.

Examine the wireless router's manual for more details.

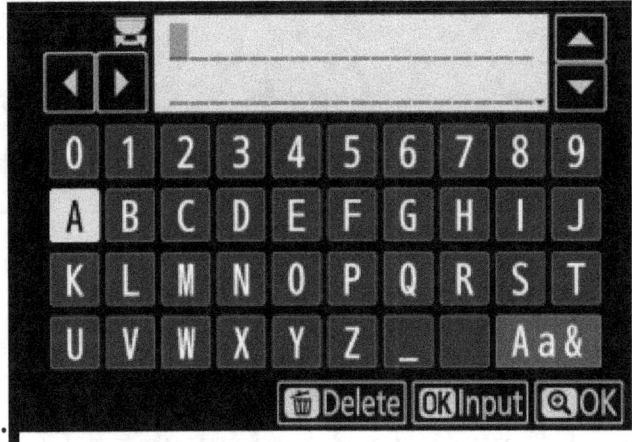

Touch X once the entry is has been completed.

To continue the call, press X once more. When the link is successfully established, a brief message will appear on screen.

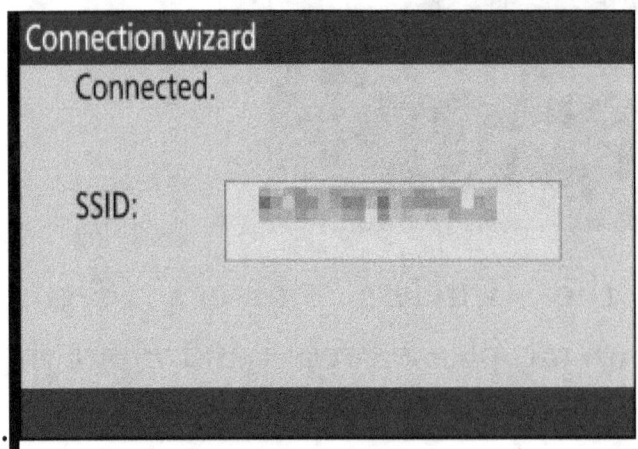

Select or get IP address.

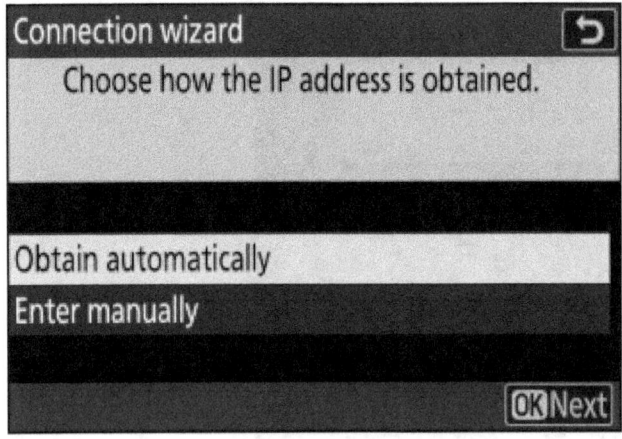

Select any of the below options and touch on J.

Option	Description
[Obtain automatically]	Select this option if the network is configured to supply the IP address automatically. A "configuration complete" message will be displayed once an IP address has been assigned.
[Enter manually]	Enter the IP address and sub-net mask manually. Press J; you will be prompted to enter the IP address. Rotate the main command dial to highlight segments. Press 4 or 2 to change the highlighted segment and press J to save changes. Next, press X; a "configuration complete" message will be displayed. Press X again to display the sub-net mask. Press 1 or 3 to edit the sub-net mask and press J; a "configuration complete" message will be displayed.

When the "configuration complete" message appears, press J to continue.

Select the kind of server.

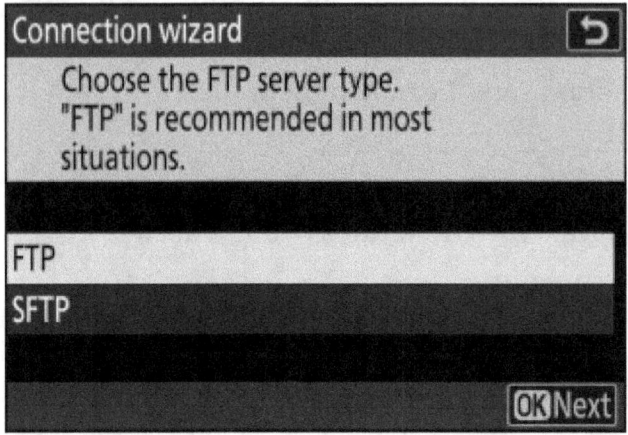

To input the server address, select [FTP] or select [SFTP] (secure FTP), then click J.

Just type in the URL of the server.

To input a server's Internet Protocol (IP) address or URL, press J.

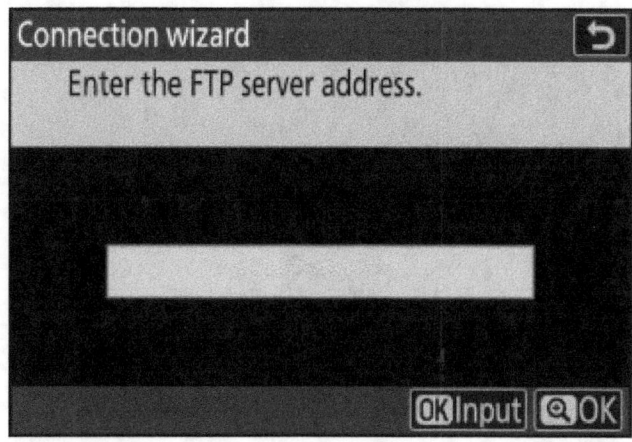

Touch X once the entry has been completed.

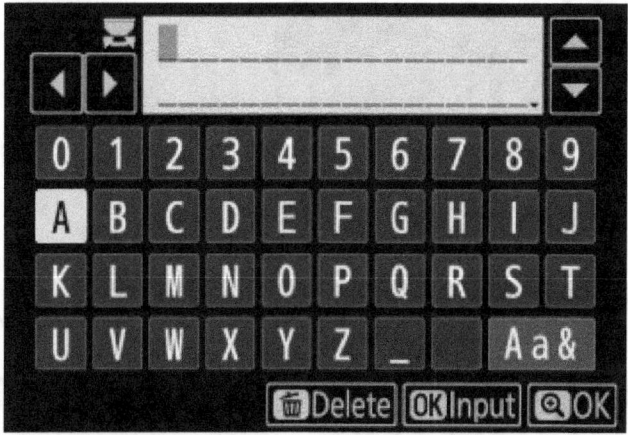

To reconnect to the FTP server, press X once again. If this is your first time logging in, you will be asked to choose your login method.

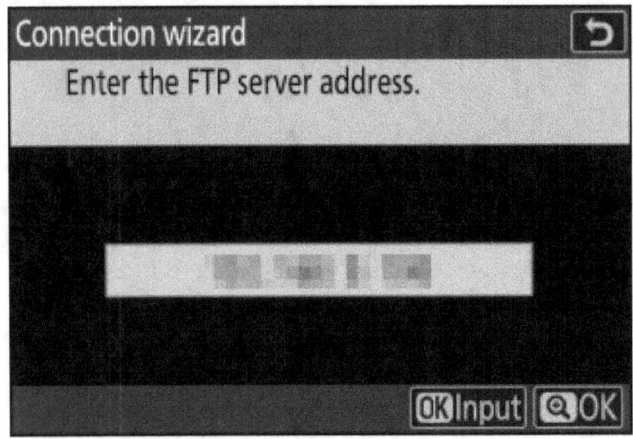

Log in.

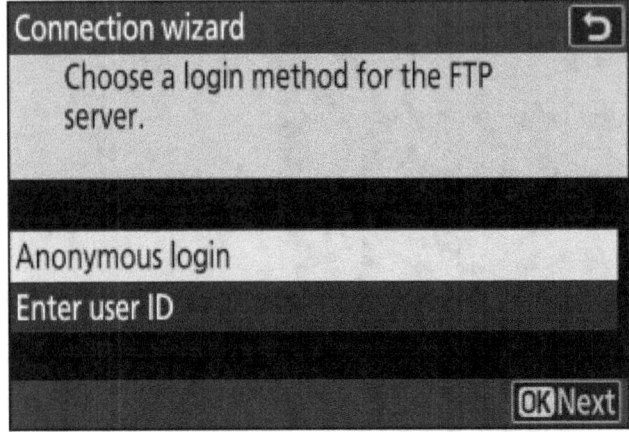

Select any of the below options and tap J.

Option	Description
[Anonymous login]	Select this option if the server does not require a user ID or password. This option can only be used with servers that are configured for anonymous login. If login is successful, the camera will prompt you to choose a destination.
[Enter user ID]	Enter a user ID and password. Press J to log in when entry is complete. If login is successful, the camera will prompt you to choose a destination.

Firewall Settings

Pick destination folder.

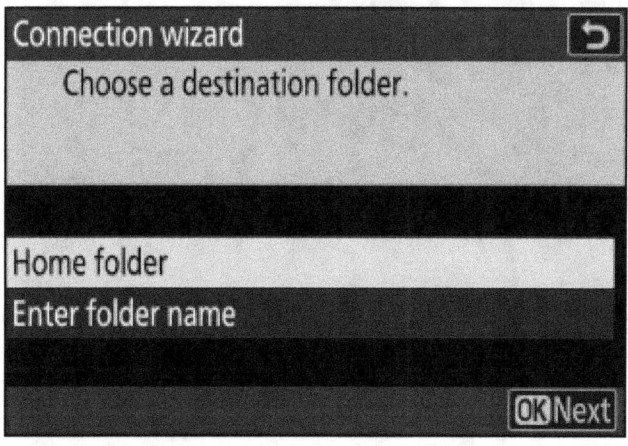

Select any of the below options and tap J.

Option	Description
[Home folder]	Select this option to select the server's home folder as the destination for pictures uploaded from the camera. A "setup complete" dialog will be displayed if the operation is successful.
[Enter folder name]	Enter the destination folder name manually. The folder must already exist on the server. Enter the folder name and path when prompted and press J to display the "setup complete" dialog.

Check connection.

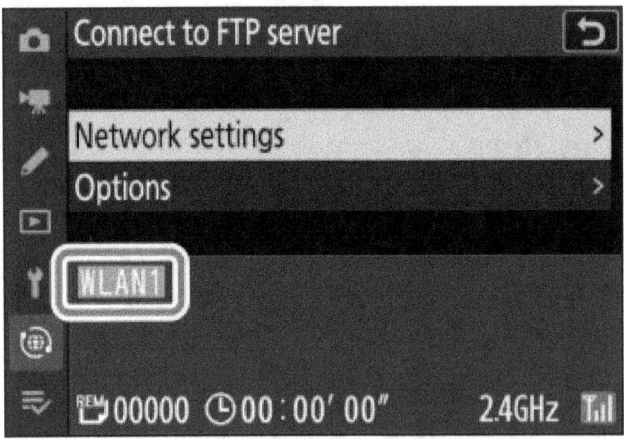

Once connected, the camera's [Connect with FTP server] option will show the profile's name in green.

The camera and FTP server may now communicate with one another wirelessly.

After taking a picture using the camera, you may transfer it to your computer over FTP as explained in "Uploading Pictures".

Ethernet

Connecting to FTP sites is possible in two ways: either directly, using the camera's built-in Ethernet port, or indirectly, via preexisting networks and an Ethernet cable of your choice.

Connect an Ethernet Plug In

The camera should be linked to a network through an Ethernet connection. Connectors should not be pushed in or inserted at an angle. Join the other end to a router or FTP server.

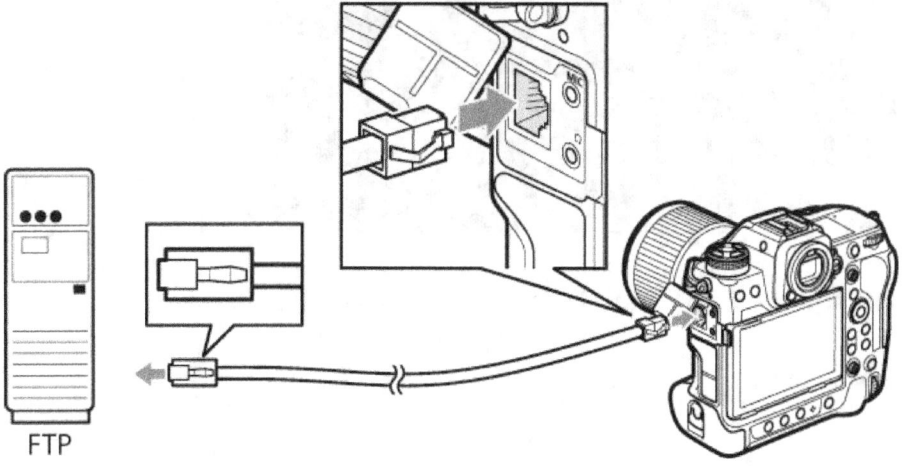

Choose [ON] for the [Wired LAN] in network menu.

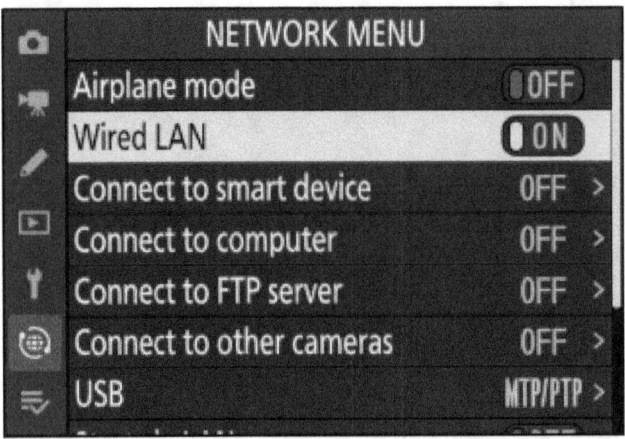

In the network menu, choose "Connect to FTP server," then select "Network settings" and hit "2.".

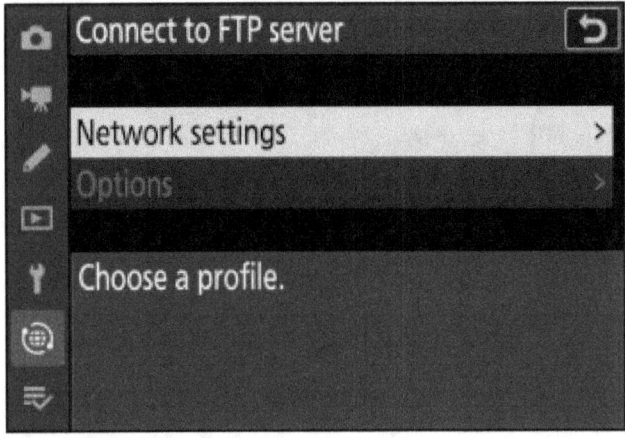

Select [Create profile] then touch J.

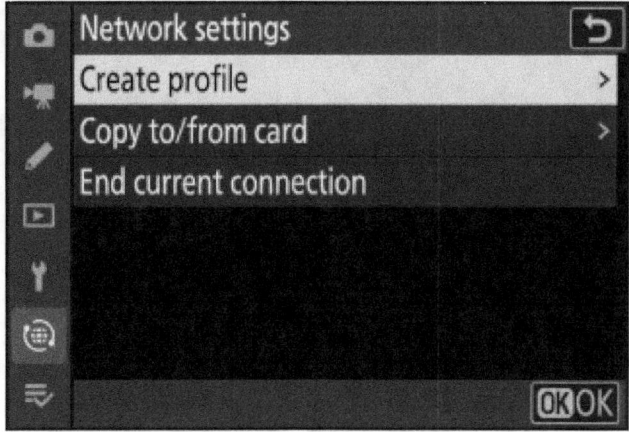

Select [Connection wizard] then touch 2.

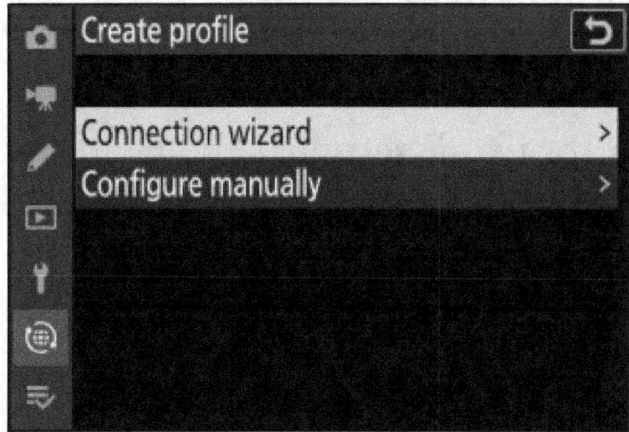

Launches connection wizard.

Manual Configuration

Rename your new profile

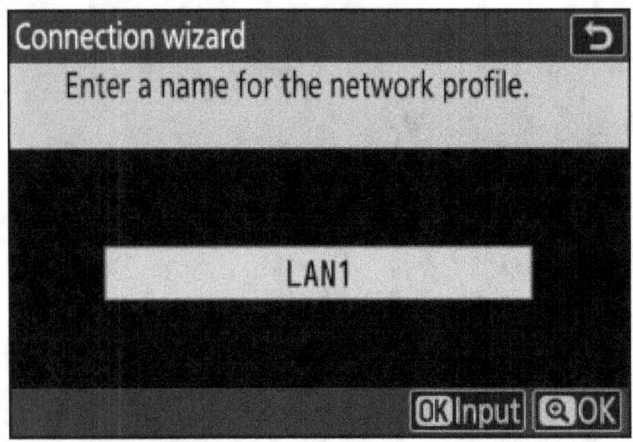

If you're OK with the default name and want to skip this stage, just hit the X.

What you call it will show up in the [Connect with FTP server] > in [Network settings] choice in the network menu.

Press J to rename the profile. Please refer to "Text Entry" for details on how to enter text (Text Entry). After a name is entered, press X to continue.

It's necessary to get an IP address, which you may either choose or be assigned.

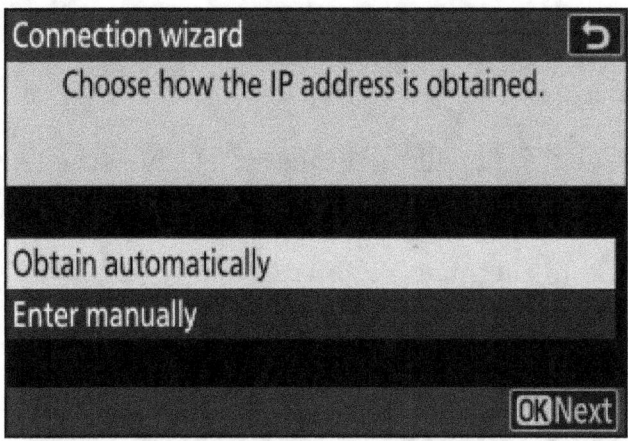

Select any of the below options then touch J.

Option	Description
[Obtain automatically]	Select this option if the network is configured to supply the IP address automatically. A "configuration complete" message will be displayed once an IP address has been assigned.

[Enter manually]	Enter the IP address and sub-net mask manually.

Press J; you will be prompted to enter the IP address.

Rotate the main command dial to highlight segments.

Press 4 or 2 to change the highlighted segment and press J to save changes.

Next, press X; a "configuration complete" message will be displayed. Press X again to display the sub-net mask.

Press 1 or 3 to edit the sub-net mask and press J; a "configuration complete" message will be displayed. |

When the "configuration complete" message appears, press J to continue.

Select the kind of server.

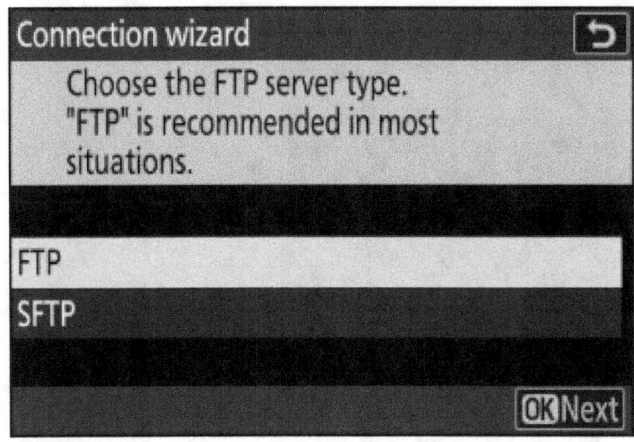

To input the server address, select [FTP] or select [SFTP] (secure FTP), then click J.

Just type in the URL of the server.

Touch J to type in the IP address or server URL

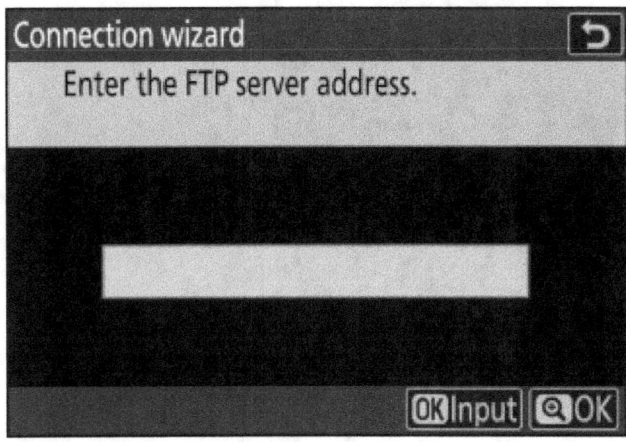

Touch X once the entry has been completed.

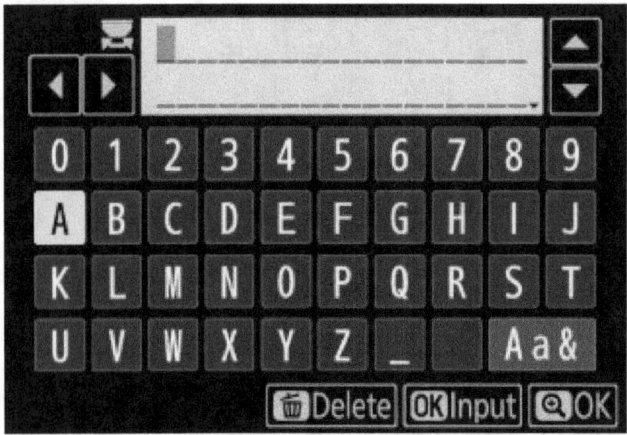

To reconnect to the FTP server, press X once again. If this is your first time logging in, you will be asked to select a login method.

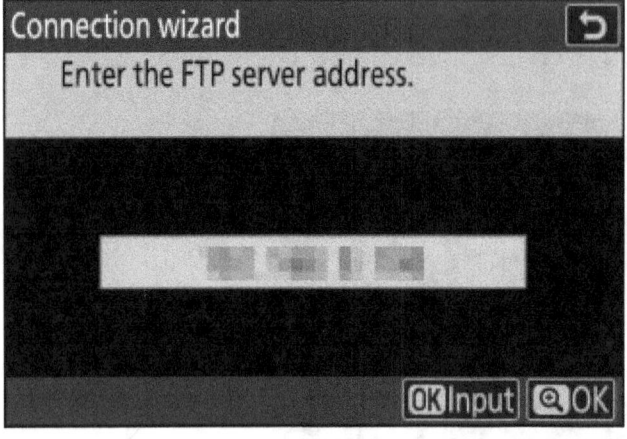

Log in.

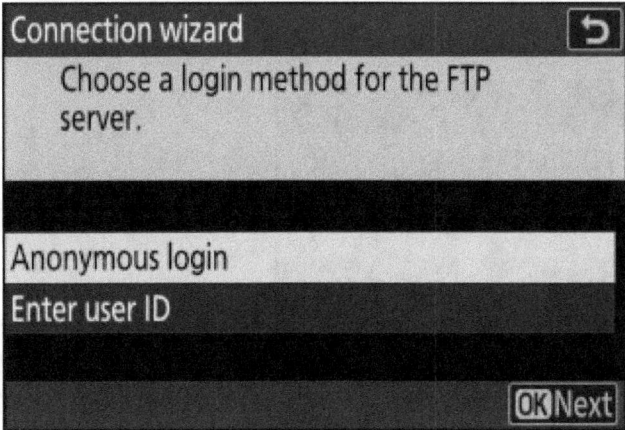

Select any of the below options and tap J.

Option	Description
[Anonymous login]	Select this option if the server does not require a user ID or password. This option can only be used with servers that are configured for anonymous login. If login is successful, the camera will prompt you to choose a destination.
[Enter user ID]	Enter a user ID and password. Press J to log in when entry is complete. If login is successful, the camera will prompt you to choose a destination.

Firewall Settings

Pick destination folder.

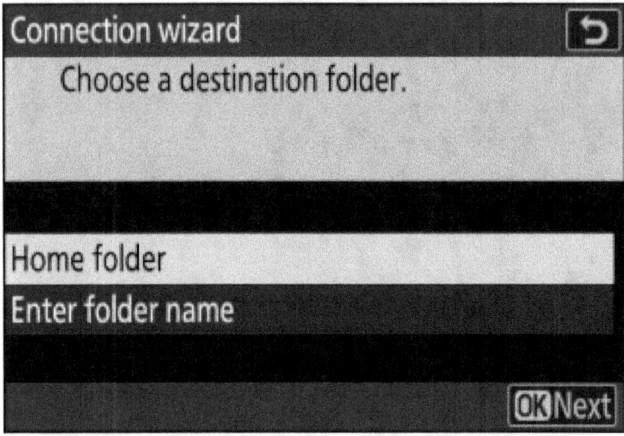

Select any of the below options and touch J.

Option	Description
[Home folder]	Select this option to select the server's home folder as the destination for pictures uploaded from the camera. A "setup complete" dialog will be displayed if the operation is successful.
[Enter folder name]	Enter the destination folder name manually. The folder must already exist on the server. Enter the folder name and path when prompted and press J to display the "setup complete" dialog.

Check connection.

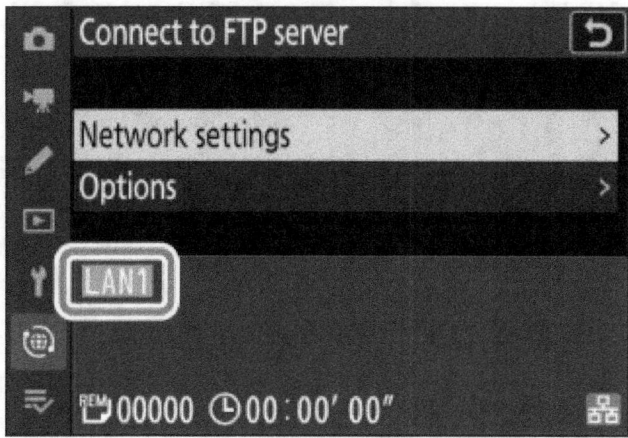

Once connected, the camera's [Connect with FTP server] option will show the profile's name in green.

The camera is now linked to the FTP server through the established connection.

After taking a picture using the camera, you may transfer it to your computer over FTP as explained in "Uploading Pictures" (Uploading Pictures).

Uploading Pictures

During the playing process, you may choose which images to submit. One other option is to have the camera upload the photos automatically as you take them.

You'll need an Ethernet cable or wireless network to link your camera to your FTP server before you can upload any photos. Make a connection by selecting a host profile under [Connect with FTP server] > [Network settings].

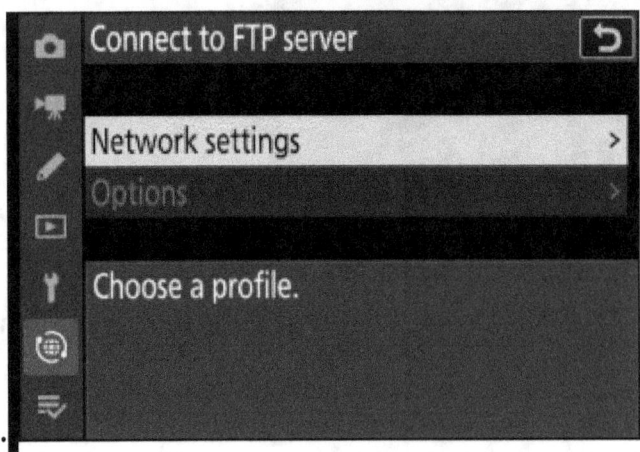

In the camera's [Connect with FTP server] menu, profile name would become green after a connection has been made.

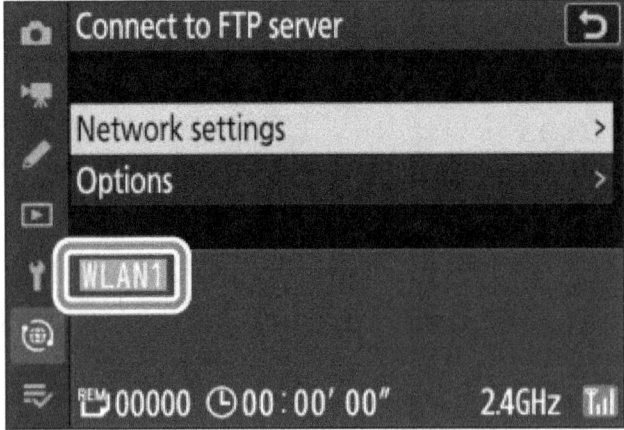

Troubleshoot Ethernet and Wireless LAN Connections

Errors that may occur via a wireless LAN or an Ethernet connection are detailed below.

Read the online documentation for Wireless Transmitter Utility to learn more about it.

Problems and Solution

Below, you'll find explanations for some frequent problems and how to fix them.

Problem	Solution
The camera displays a wireless error.	Connection settings require adjustment. Check settings for the wireless router, FTP server, or host computer and adjust camera settings appropriately (Wireless LAN, Wireless LAN).
The camera displays a TCP/IP error. The camera displays an FTP error.	Check the error code, if any. For more information, see "Error Codes" (Error Codes).

"Connecting to computer" does not clear from the camera display.	Check firewall settings (Firewall Settings, Firewall Settings).
The camera displays the message, "Ethernet cable is not connected".	Connect an Ethernet cable or select [OFF] for [Wired LAN] (Ethernet Connections, Ethernet, Wired LAN).
The camera displays a "no memory card" error.	The memory card is inserted incorrectly or not at all. Check that card is inserted correctly (Inserting Memory Cards).
Upload is interrupted and fails to resume.	Upload will resume if the camera is turned off and then on again (Loss of Signal).

Error Codes

If an issue arises when an FTP server is connected to your camera through Ethernet or a wireless LAN, the following warnings and error codes may be shown.

Wireless Error

Error code	Solution
Err. 11	Confirm that the device to which you are attempting to connect is on.
	Check the SSID (Connect to FTP Server).
Err. 12	Confirm that you are using the correct password for the selected SSID.
	Confirm that you are using the correct authentication method (Connect to FTP Server).

Error code	Solution
Err. 13	Confirm that the device to which you are attempting to connect is on.
	Turn the camera off and then on again.
Err. 1F	Turn the camera off and then on again.

[TCP/IP Error.]

Error code	Solution
Err. 21	Check that the TCP/IP address and sub-net mask are correct (Connect to FTP Server).
Err. 22	Duplicate TCP/IP address. Choose a different address (Connect to FTP Server).

[PTP/IP Error.]

Error code	Solution
Err. 41	Turn the camera off and then on again.

[FTP Error.]

Error code	Solution
Err. 31	Check that the FTP server address is correct (Connect to FTP Server).
Err. 32	Check that the login name and password are correct (Connect to FTP Server).
Err. 34	Check that the destination folder name is correct (Connect to FTP Server).
Err. 35	Confirm that the destination folder is not write-protected.
Err. 36	Check the DNS (Connect to FTP Server).

Error code	Solution
Err. 37	Check firewall settings (Firewall Settings).
	Check PASV mode settings (Connect to FTP Server).
Err. 3F	Turn the camera off and then on again.

Camera to camera connection

Benefits include'

Camera Remote Photography (Sync Release)

The shutters of up to ten individual cameras in same group may be triggered by a single master camera (Synchronized Release)

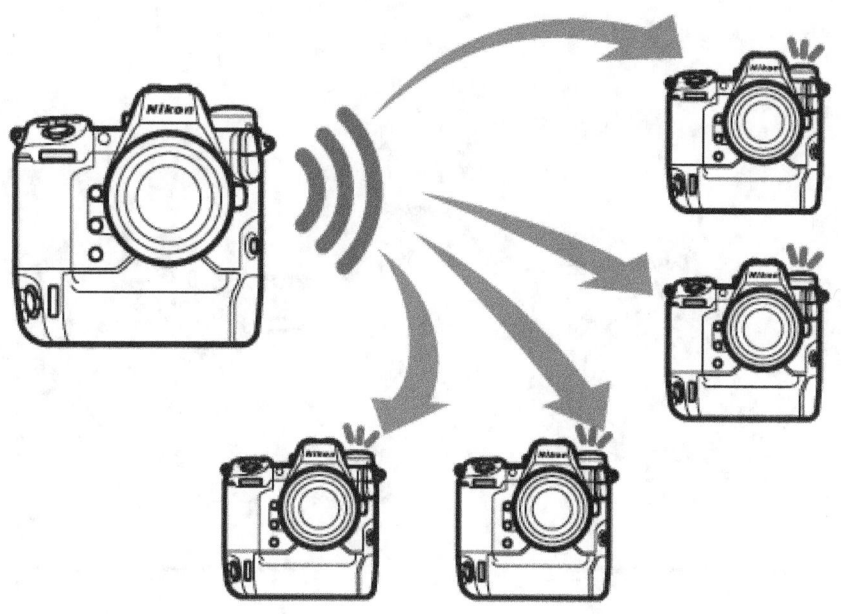

Clock Sync (Date & Time)

Connected cameras may share the same time stamps by coordinating their clocks (Synchronizing Camera Clocks).

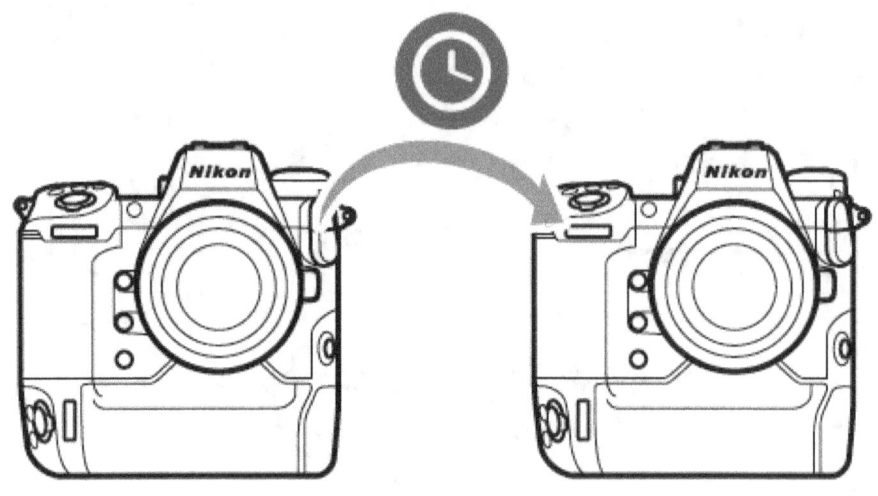

Configure and use Sync Release

To create a host profile for a simultaneous release, follow the instructions below. The photos taken by each camera are stored on their own memory card. To ensure that all cameras end up with similar profiles, just start again.

Wireless LAN

When using a wireless LAN, follow these steps to set up a host profile:

In the Network menu, choose "Connect to other cameras," then select "Network settings" and click "2.".

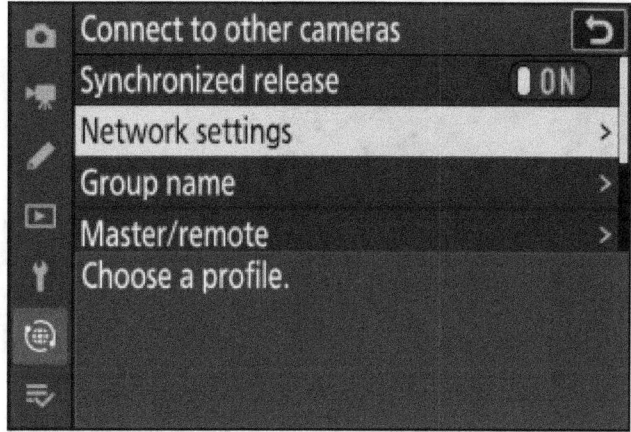

Select [Create profile] then tap J.

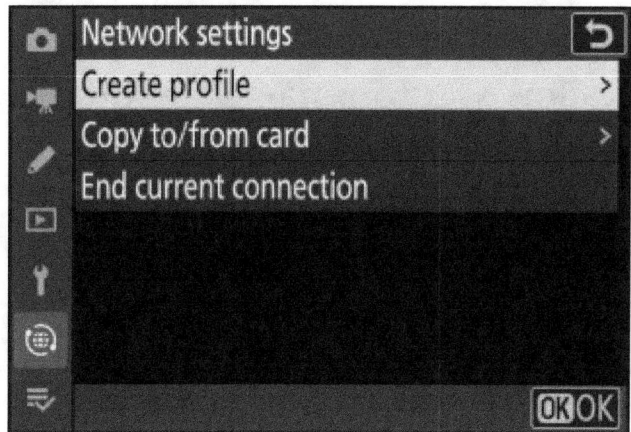

Title your new profile.

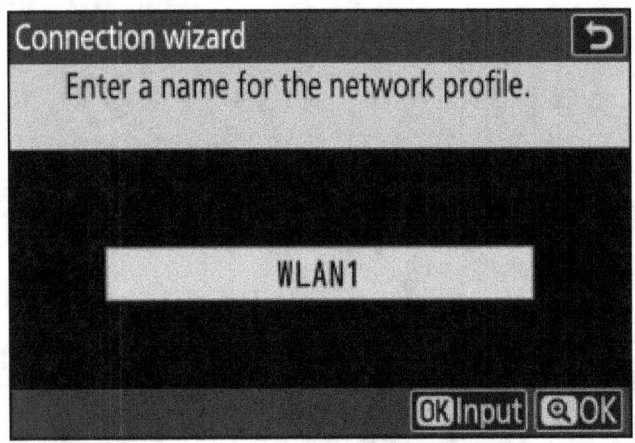

If you're OK with the default name and want to skip this stage, just hit the X.

The name you give it will be shown in the [Connect other cameras] > [Network settings] menu.

The letter J will allow you to rename the profile. Please refer to "Text Entry" for more on this topic (Text Entry). After a name is entered, press X to continue.

Select "Search wireless networks" and hit "J".

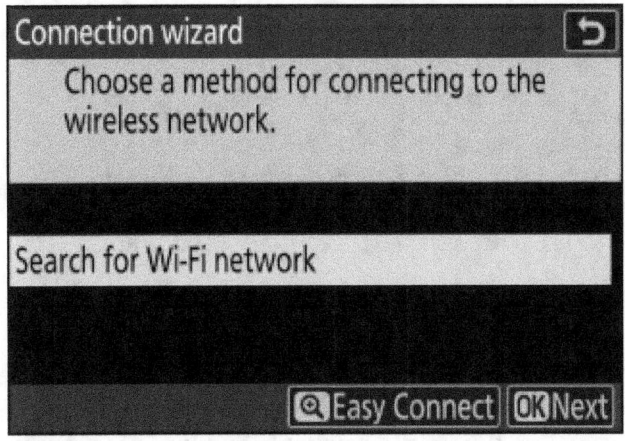

The camera will scan the area for any nearby networks and provide a list of them (SSID).

Easy Connect

Select network.

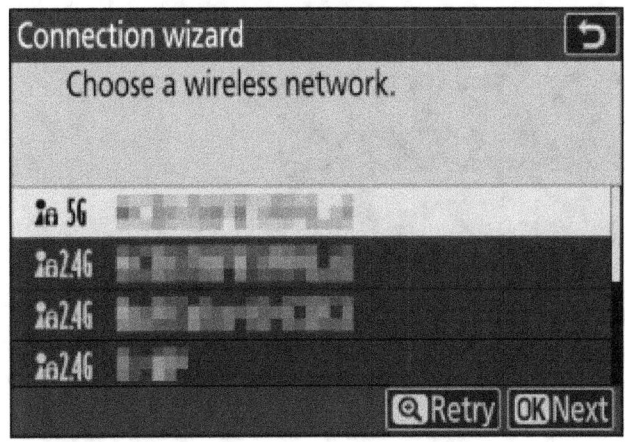

Select network SSID then touch J.

Each SSID has an associated icon that represents the frequency range across which it operates.

The h symbol denotes a secure connection. The encryption key will be requested if the network you've chosen (h) requires it. Step 7 should be performed if network isn't encrypted.

Select X to do a new network search if the one you want isn't shown.

Hidden SSIDs

Type in encryption key.

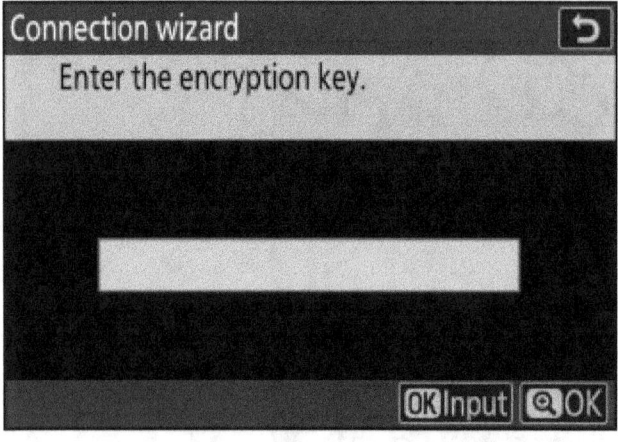

Tap J and type in the wireless router encryption key.

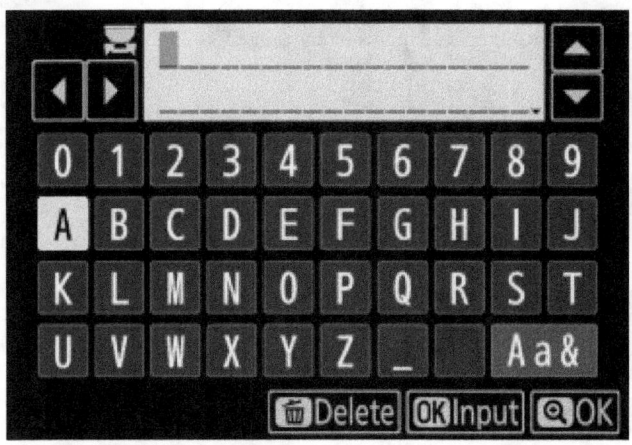

When finished, please press the X.

You may restart the link by pressing X one again. When the link is successfully established, a message will appear on screen for a little period of time.

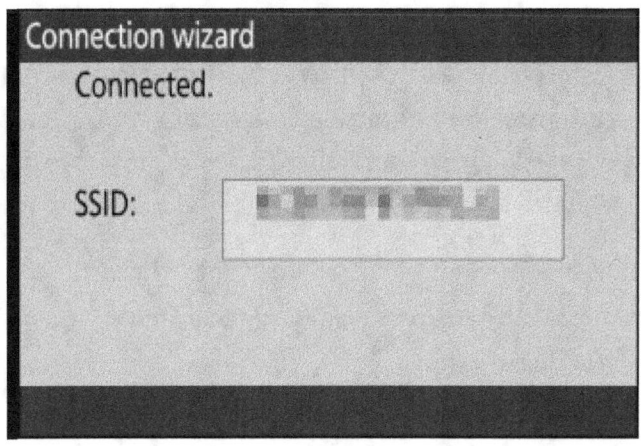

Get or choose IP address.

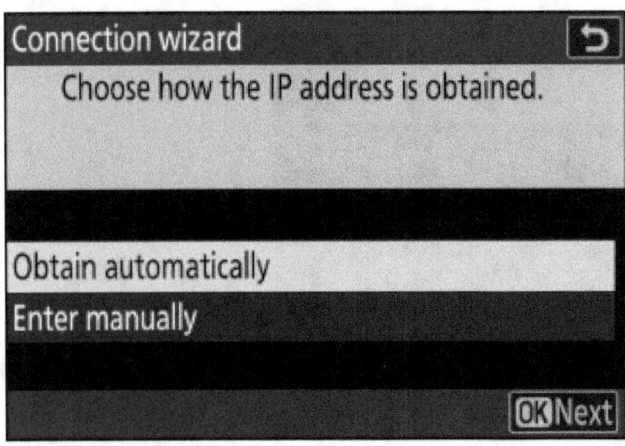

Select any of the below options and touch J.

Option	Description
[Obtain automatically]	Select this option if the network is configured to supply the IP address automatically. A "configuration complete" message will be displayed once an IP address has been assigned. It is recommended that you note the remote camera IP address, as you will need it in subsequent steps.

Option	Description
[Enter manually]	Enter the IP address and sub-net mask manually. Press J; you will be prompted to enter the IP address. Rotate the main command dial to highlight segments. Press 4 or 2 to change the highlighted segment and press J to save changes. Next, press X; a "configuration complete" message will be displayed. Press X again to display the sub-net mask. Press 1 or 3 to edit the sub-net mask and press J; a "configuration complete" message will be displayed.

In order to continue after the "configuration complete" message has been shown, press J.

Whenever a connection is made, profile name is shown.

To create a new group, select the [Group name] box, then press 2.

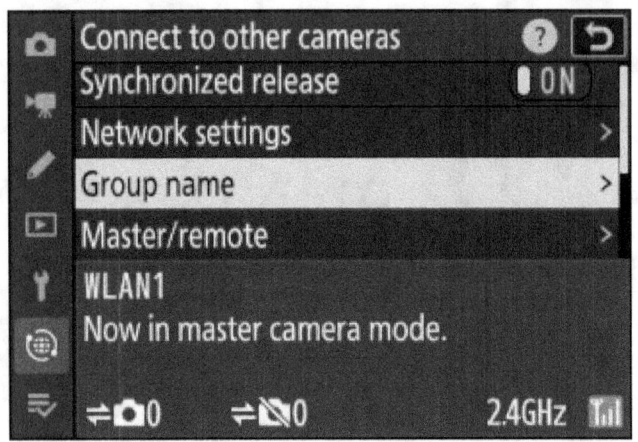

Give the grouped cameras a name. There's a limit of eight characters for a group's name.

All network cameras, both master and slave, need to be part of the same group.

Select [Master/remote], and then press 2.

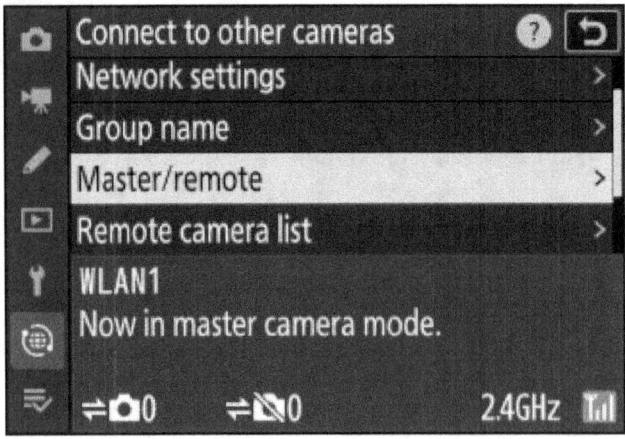

If you're using several cameras, you'll need to assign each one a "master" or "remote" function.

When the shutter release button on master camera is pressed, all of the other cameras' shutters are also allowed to open. There may be only one leader for each given organization. Even if more than one master camera exists in a given group, only the first one to successfully join the network will be used in that role.

[Remote camera] All of the cameras' shutters are timed to fire at the exact same moment as the master camera.

Steps 1–9 must be repeated for each camera that remains.

In Step 9, choose [Remote camera] to configure remote cameras.

In order to access the remote cameras, press 2 on the main camera after selecting [Remote camera list].

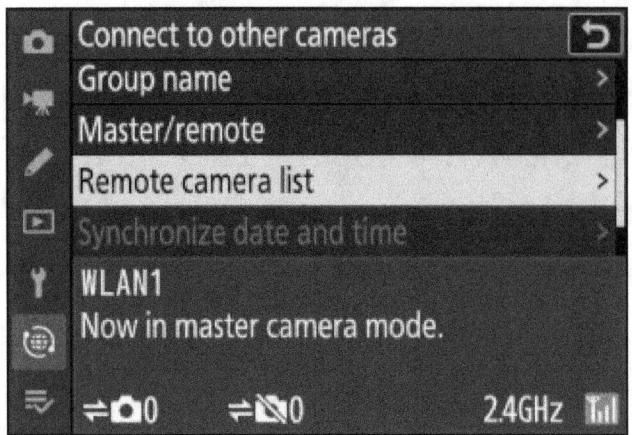

In Step 9, cameras that will function as remote cameras are included to master camera's remote camera list. In slots [01] thru [10], the master camera may save data for a total of ten additional cameras.

Select the desired option and hit the 2 button.

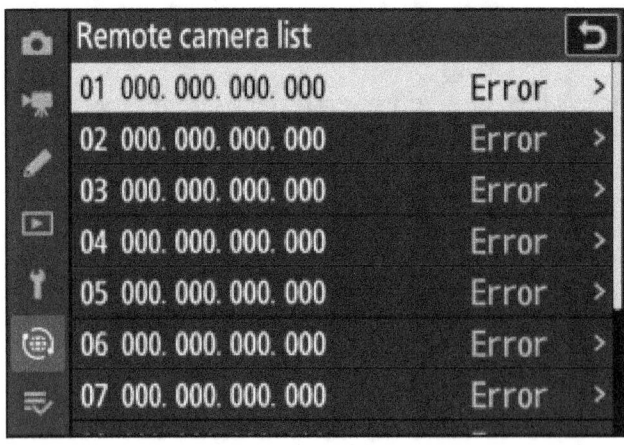

Options for Remote camera will be Shown.

Select [Address] and touch 2.

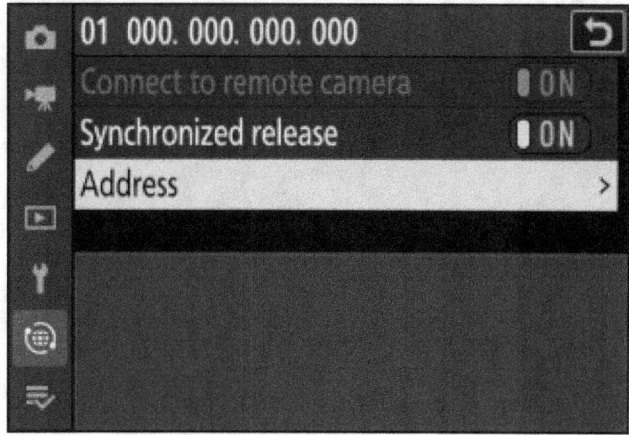

An IP address input field will appear.

Type in the IP address of the distant camera.

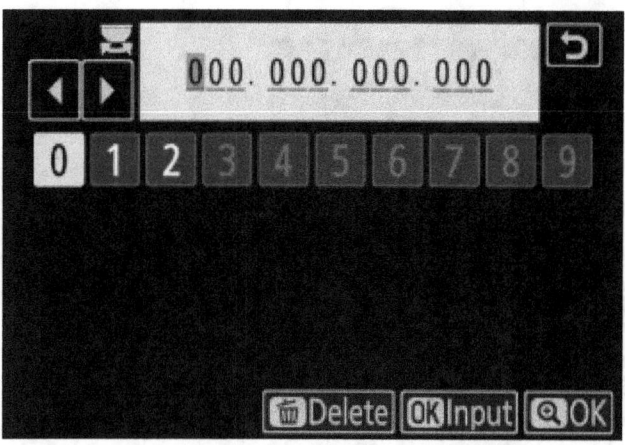

Go ahead and type in the IP address of the remote camera you wrote down in Step 7.

To bring up other sections, just rotate the main control dial.

Alter the selected text by pressing 4 or 2 and then press J to continue.

To connect remote camera to master camera, press the X button.

Add the other remote camera

The cameras will show the band utilized by the chosen SSID when you connect to wireless networks.

The number of linked and unconnected cameras in the cluster is shown on the master camera.

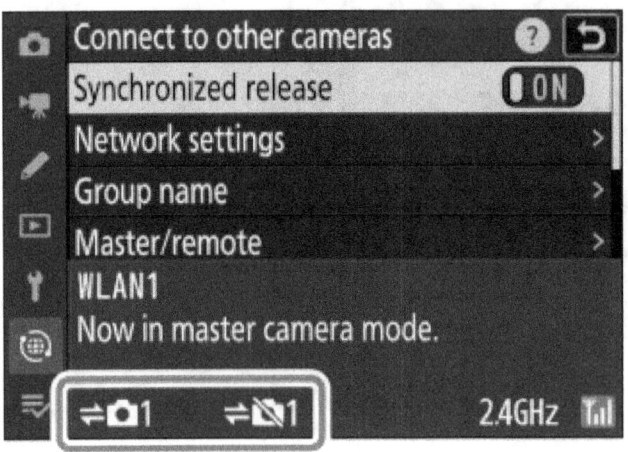

Take pictures.

When the shutter button is pressed on the main camera, all of the other cameras in the system will open as well.

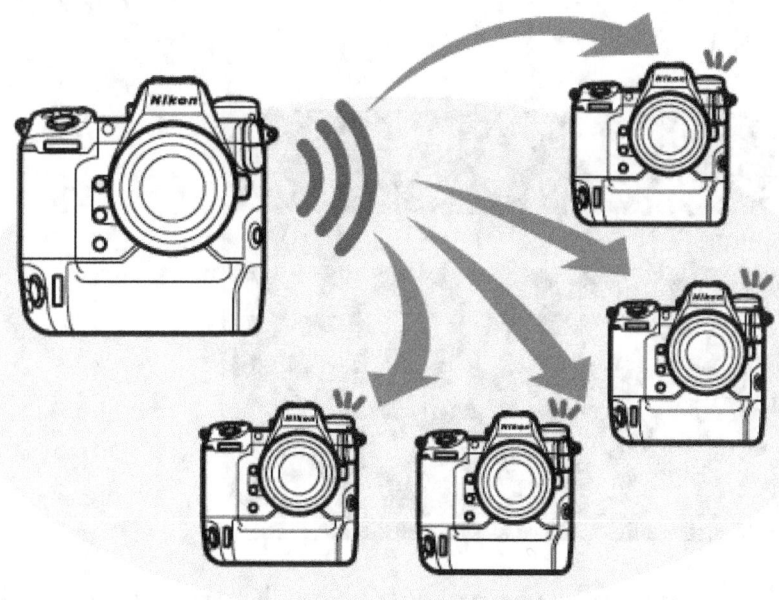

Keep in mind that when cameras are in sync release mode, the standby timers will not automatically run out.

Ethernet

Create a host profile for your Ethernet connection by following the instructions below. In order to go further, an Ethernet cable must be plugged into the camera's Ethernet port. Do not try to push the connections in or insert them at an angle. Connect the cable's opposite end to a network switch or hub.

To activate [Wired LAN] in network settings, set it to [ON].

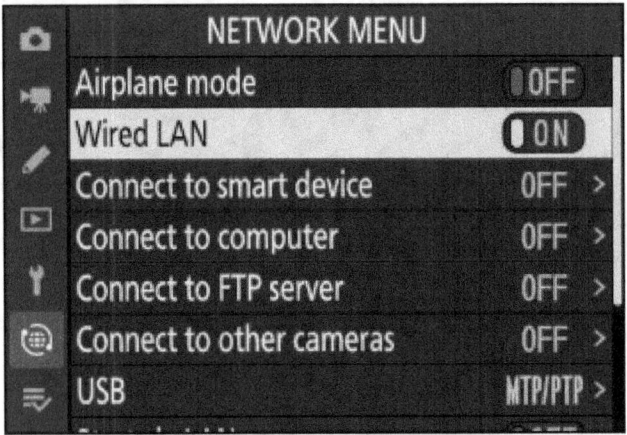

In the Network menu, choose "Connect to other cameras," then select "Network settings" and click "2.".

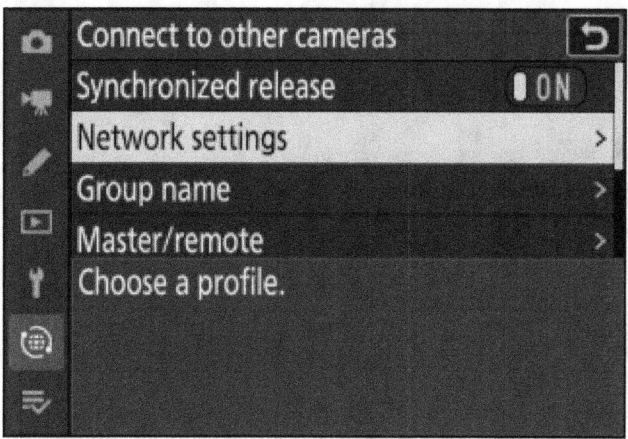

Select [Create profile] then touch J.

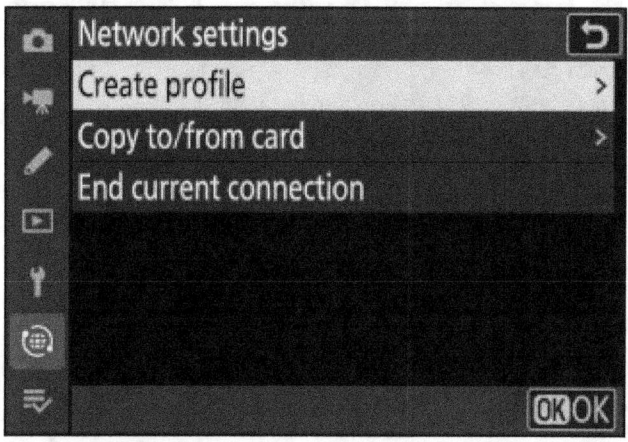

Name profile.

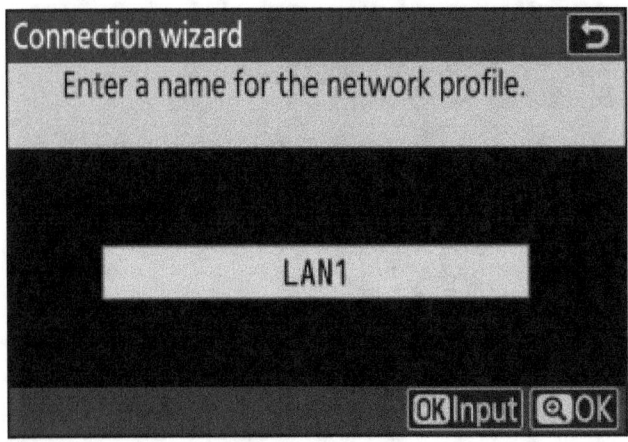

If you don't want to alter the default name, pressing X will bring you further IP address choices.

The name you give it will be shown in the [Connect other cameras] > [Network settings] menu.

The letter J will allow you to rename the profile. Please refer to "Text Entry" for more on this topic (Text Entry). After a name is entered, press X to continue.

Get or decide on an IP address.

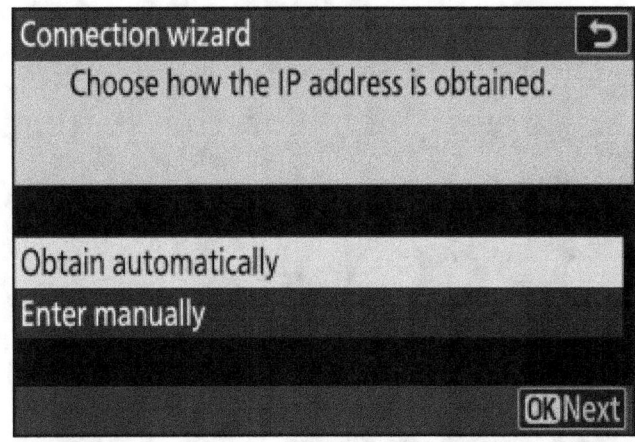

Select any of the below options and touch J.

Option	Description
[Obtain automatically]	Select this option if the network is configured to supply the IP address automatically. A "configuration complete" message will be displayed once an IP address has been assigned. It is recommended that you note the remote camera IP address, as you will need it in subsequent steps.

In order to continue after the "configuration complete" message has been shown, press J.

When a link is made, profile name is shown.

To create a new group, highlight the [Group name] box, then press 2.

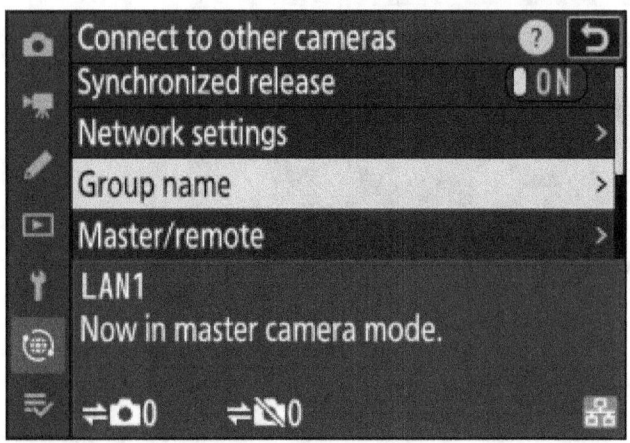

Give the grouped cameras a name. There's a limit of eight characters for a group's name.

All network cameras, both master and slave, must belong to the same group.

Select [Master/remote], and then press 2.

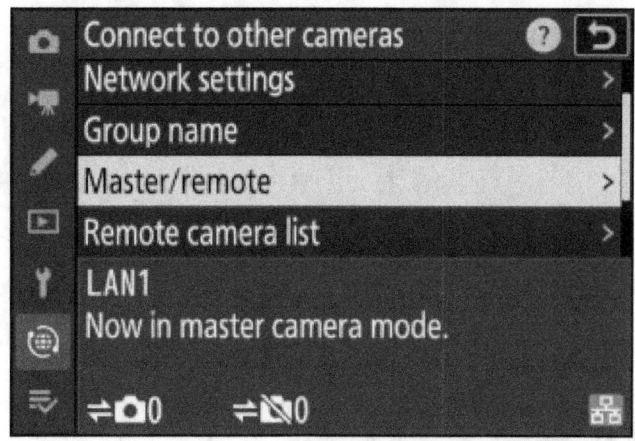

If you're using several cameras, you'll need to assign each one a "master" or "remote" function.

When the shutter release button in master camera is pressed, all of the other cameras' shutters are also allowed to open. There may be only one leader for each given organization. Even if more than one master camera exists in a given group, only the first one to successfully join the network will be used in that role.

[Remote camera] All of the cameras' shutters are timed to fire at the exact same moment as the master camera.

Steps 1-7 must be repeated for each additional camera.

Pick [Remote camera] at Step 7 if you're setting up a camera from afar.

In order to access the remote cameras, press 2 on the main camera after selecting [Remote camera list].

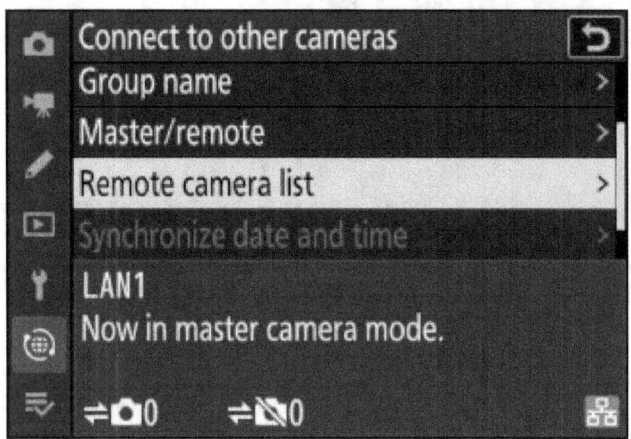

In Step 7, cameras are given the remote camera role and added to the remote camera list on the master camera. In slots [01] thru [10], the master camera may save data for a total of ten additional cameras.

Select the desired option and hit the 2 button.

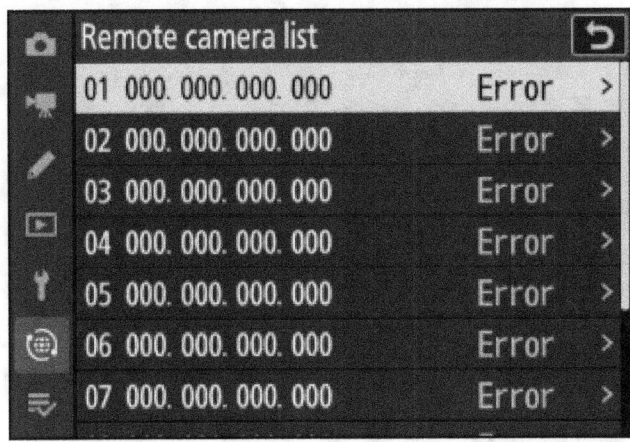

Options for Remote camera will be shown.

Flash Photography

"On-Camera" Vs "Remote"

The camera's accessory shoe may accommodate a flash unit, or you can use one or more separate flash units, both of which are available as an option.

Flashes should have [Silent mode] set to [OFF] in the configuration menu.

Mounted Camera Flash Units

Use the camera's built-in flash to take images. More details may be found on the following pages (Using On-Camera Flash).

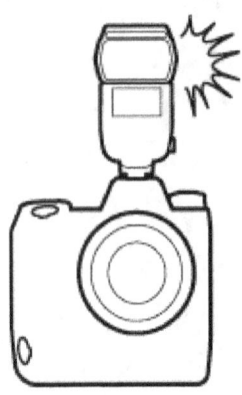

Remote Flash Photography

Use wireless flash control to snap shots utilizing one or more off-camera flashes (Advanced Wireless Lighting). See "Remote Flash Photography" for details (Remote Flash Photography).

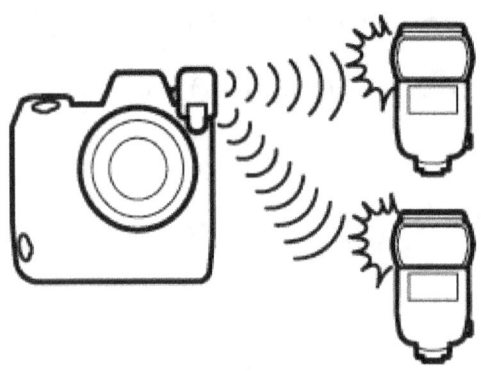

Use On-Camera Flash

On your cam accessory shoe, you can Mount a flash unit.

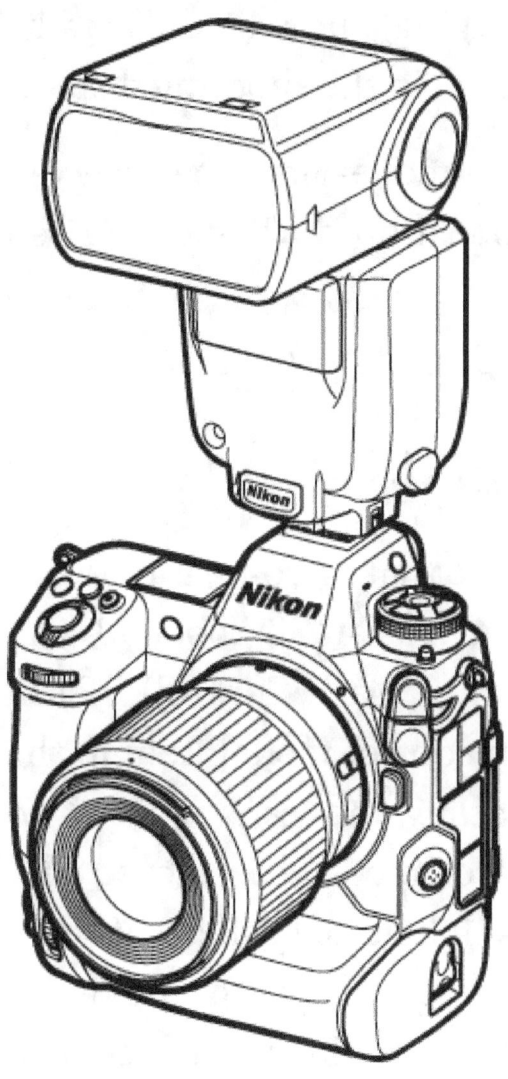

In order to learn how to attach the Speedlight to the camera, read the included instructions.

Please turn the camera and flash unit on.

The flash will start charging, and when it's ready, you'll see an indication (c) in the shooting display.

Flash modes and flash modes may be selected from Flash Control Mode drop-down menu (Flash Modes).

Adjust the aperture and shutter speed.

Flash Control Mode

When using a flash unit that is compatible with unified flash control (such as an SB-5000, SB-500, SB-400, or SB 300; Unified Flash Control), [Flash control] > select [Flash control mode] item in the menu for photo shooting and can be used to change the flash control mode, flash level, and other flash settings. Each kind of flash has its own unique set of options for adjusting the light. Depending on what you choose for [Flash control mode], the display for adjusting the flash will change its available settings.

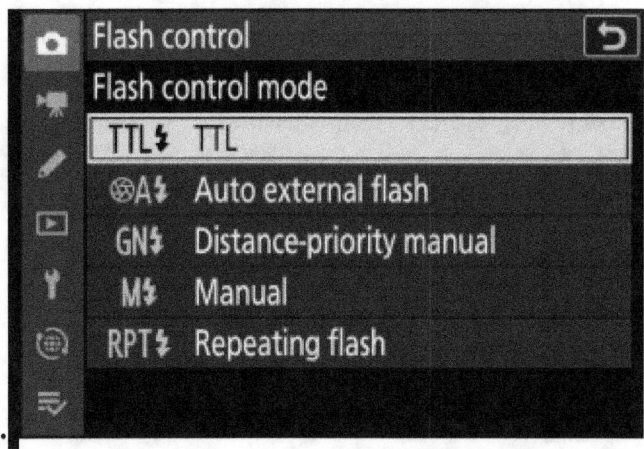

Controls on the flash unit itself are the sole way to change flash units settings other than SB-500, SB-5000, SB-400, as well as SB 300.

Adjusting the flash's settings is as simple as using the unit's buttons, which can be used for the SB-5000 even while it's attached to the shoe.

Option	Description
[TTL]	Flash output is adjusted automatically in response to shooting conditions. Output can be adjusted using [Flash compensation (TTL)].
[Auto external flash]	Light from the flash is reflected from the subject to an auto external flash sensor and flash output adjusted automatically. Output can be adjusted using [Auto external flash compensation]. Auto external flash supports "auto aperture" (qA) and "non-TTL auto" (A) modes. For details, see the documentation provided with the flash unit.

Option	Description
[Distance-priority manual]	Choose the distance to the subject; flash output will be adjusted automatically. The distance to the subject is selected using [Distance-priority options] > [Distance], while flash output can be adjusted using [Flash compensation].
[Manual]	Choose the flash level manually. Flash output is selected using [Manual output amount].

Flash Modes

Hold C button & turn the dial for main command to select flash mode.

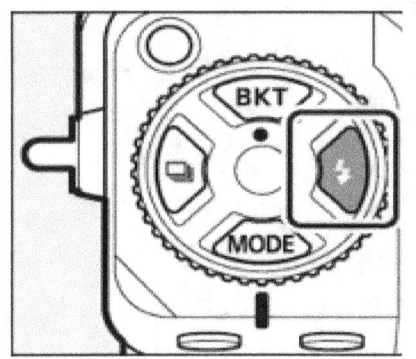 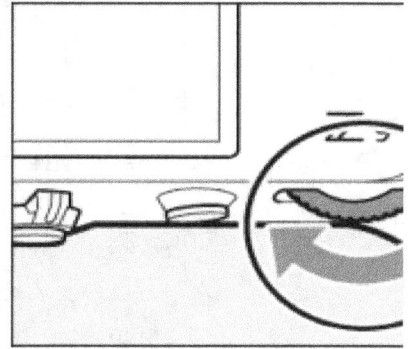

Option	Description	Available in
I [Fill flash] (front-curtain sync)	This mode is recommended in most situations. In modes P and A, shutter speed will automatically be set to values between 1/200 s (or 1/8000 s with auto FP high-speed sync) and 1/60 s.	P, S, A, M

Option		Description	Available in
J	[Red-eye reduction]	Use for portraits. The flash fires before the photograph is taken, reducing "red-eye". A flash unit with red-eye reduction is required. The desired results may not be achieved if the subject or camera moves before the shutter is released (this setting is not recommended with moving subjects or in other situations requiring a quick shutter response).	P, S, A, M
L	[Slow sync]	As for "fill flash", except that shutter speed slows automatically to capture background lighting at night or under low light. Note that photos may be prone to blurring due to camera shake at slow shutter speeds. Use of a tripod is recommended.	P, A

FV Lock

For alternative CLS-compatible flash units, you can lock flash output to capture many photographs or recompose without adjusting the flash intensity. There is greater leeway in how you arrange photos if your subject isn't dead center.

The brightness of the flash will adapt automatically to variations in ISO and aperture.

Custom Setting f2 may be used to designate a switch as a [FV lock]. [Firearms with User-Defined Controls].

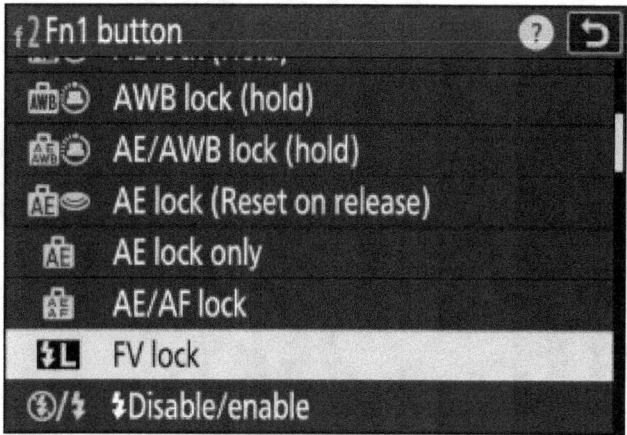

Attach an FV-lock capable flash to the camera's shoe.

Power on the flash and choose TTL or the monitor pre-flash A or qA for flash control.

Select [TTL] or [Auto external flash] from [Flash control] > [Flash control mode] if you have SB-5000, SB-500, SB-400, or SB-300 attached to the camera's hot shoe.

Refer to the user manual for further information on how to use the device and how to change the flash settings.

Focus

The subject should be centered in the picture, and the shutter release button should be depressed halfway to focus.

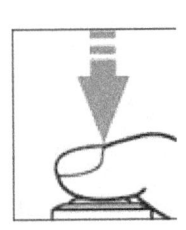
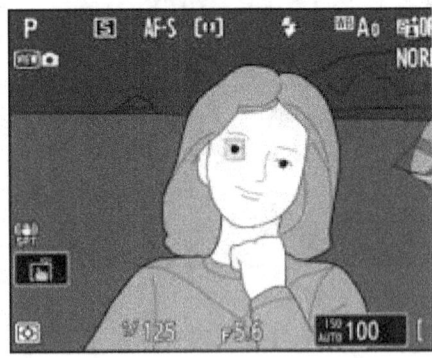

Lock flash level.

Once you've checked that the flash-ready indication (c) has shown in the shooting display, you may click the [FV lock] button to trigger a monitor pre-flash from the flash unit, which will help you gauge the optimal flash intensity.

A FV lock icon (r) would show in the viewfinder after the flash output has been locked.

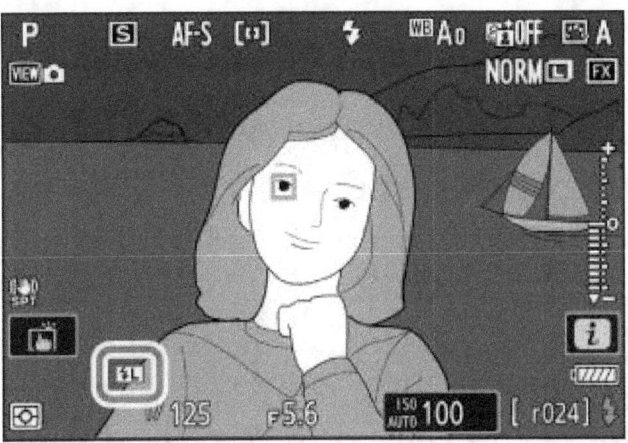

Recompose shot.

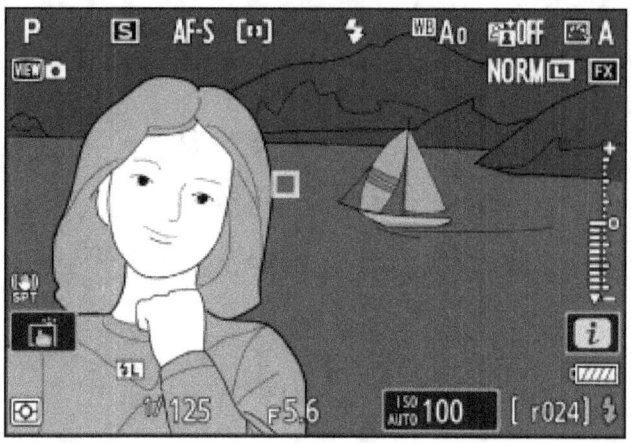

The last half-press of the shutter-release button is required for a shot.

Additional shots may be taken without disabling FV lock if desired. Additional photographs may be taken by repeating Steps 6 and 7.

Remove the FV Lock

To remove FV lock, press the [FV lock] button and make sure FV lock icon (r) has disappeared from the shooting display.

www.ingramcontent.com/pod-product-compliance
Lightning Source LLC
Chambersburg PA
CBHW071405210526
45465CB00001B/257